Battling the Prince of Darkness

To dearest David & La Verne

Love, Evelyn

Battling the Prince of Darkness

Evelyn Christenson

While this book is intended for the reader's personal enjoyment and profit, it is also intended for group study. A leader's guide with Reproducible Response Sheets is available from your local bookstore or from the publisher.

VICTOR BOOKS ®

A DIVISION OF SCRIPTURE PRESS PUBLICATIONS INC.
USA CANADA ENGLAND

Unless otherwise noted, Scripture quotations are from *New American Standard Bible*, © the Lockman Foundation 1960, 1962, 1963, 1968, 1971, 1972, 1973, 1975, 1977. Quotations marked (KJV) are from the King James Version.

Library of Congress Cataloging-in-Publication Data

Christenson, Evelyn.
    Battling the Prince of Darkness / by Evelyn Christenson.
        p.   cm
    ISBN 0-89693-251-6
    1. Devil. 2. Satanism. 3. Evangelistic work. I. Title.
    BT981.C48   1990
    235'.4—dc20   90-34878
                                                              CIP

    3   4   5   6   7   8   9   10   Printing/Year   94   93   92   91

CONTENTS

ONE
THE LOST DOCTRINE
Colossians 1:13

A new spiritual battle is raging on planet Earth. Forces of good and evil are vying openly as never before for the minds and souls of human beings. Pastors, missionaries, and lay Christians are bombarding me these days with their stories of almost unbelievable attacks from the Prince of Darkness.

What can Christians do about today's terrible explosion of satanic activity, Satan worship, occult practices, and the New Age movement?

Must we helplessly watch as these emissaries of Satan's kingdom brainwash our children through occult-oriented TV programs and comic books? Or agonize while they infiltrate our schools, television, government, and military with their anti-God philosophies, witchcraft, and even satanic worship? Must we ignore the occult themes saturating our teen's electronic games? Must we turn a deaf ear to the hard rock music that actually explains and encourages satanic rituals, diabolical sex practices, and even suicide? Must Christians only recoil in shock as Satan worshipers sacrifice human adults and breed babies to sacrifice to their god?

Must we tolerate the evil producing our uncontrollable drug abuse, skyrocketing crime, rampant violence, sexual child abuse, pornography, family breakdown, and loss of integrity in government? Is there no hope for a victory against evil? No power against it?

Must Christians sit idly by, increasingly horrified, and accept Satan's attacks on all we hold dear?

Must we always be on the defensive—just trying to protect ourselves from this onslaught? Or is there an offensive attack possible for us? Is there a way we can mobilize *our* forces and offensively attack Satan's forces? Do Christians have the answer?

THE LOST DOCTRINE

Yes, Christians do have an answer. In fact, we have the *only* answer. The reason all this evil is taking place has its roots in what happened to our first parents in the Garden of Eden.

It was then that Satan, having been cast out of heaven for his sin, pitted himself against God for the allegiance of the first human beings. And when Adam and Eve fell into his grasp, the Bible tells us *they took the whole human race with them into Satan's evil kingdom.*

So then as through one transgression there resulted condemnation to all men (Romans 5:18).

But most Christian churches seem to have lost, or at least have let slip out of their teaching, the very doctrine that holds the key to this recent evil explosion—the "doctrine of original sin." Some churches have openly replaced it with psychology's answer that everybody is born good—until something happens to make them turn bad. Other churches have just let the doctrine of original sin slip away and die a natural death.

Although this doctrine of original sin is in the official tenents of every major denomination and independent church today, it is an unsettling doctrine. It is uncomfortable to look at all people without Jesus as lost—and in Satan's kingdom. So human plans and programs have largely replaced it. And that is our problem today. We have the key to the disaster of original sin, but we are not using it.

TRANSFERRED CITIZENSHIP

Are you eagerly asking, "Well, what *is* the key?" It is very simple. *Win them to Jesus!*

What really happens when someone is won to Jesus? Actually, that person is transferred from one kingdom to another. These kingdoms are spiritual, and there are only two of them in the universe. These kingdoms have rulers—locked in mortal combat for the souls of people. *So soul winning in evangelism is getting involved in the battle between the rulers of the two spiritual kingdoms of the universe for the souls of people on planet Earth.*

These two kingdoms are the "kingdom of darkness" ruled by Satan and the "kingdom of God's Son Jesus Christ."

The Bible makes this transferring of citizenship from the Prince of Darkness' kingdom to Jesus' kingdom very clear in Colossians 1:13:

> For He [the Father] delivered us from the *domain of darkness* and transferred us to the *kingdom of His beloved Son.*

Today there is a new intensity in the war for souls that began in the Garden of Eden. But we Christians have the key. Accepting Jesus makes a new creation of these lost ones—with new priorities, attitudes, and actions. As members of God's holy kingdom they have His power to change from their evil lifestyles to lifestyles reflecting peace and love in Jesus.

UNFAIR ADVANTAGE

However, it seems that the ruler of one of these kingdoms has an unfair advantage, since every person born on earth *automatically* is a citizen of his kingdom. From the fall of Adam and Eve until now, everyone on planet Earth has been born into Satan's kingdom.

In Romans 5:12 through 21 we are told why all people are born already condemned. It was Adam and Eve's first sin in the Garden of Eden that put all humans born after them in Satan's kingdom—condemned to spiritual and physical death.

Therefore, just as through one man sin entered into the world, and death through sin, and so death spread to all men, because all sinned (Romans 5:12).

For on the one hand the judgment arose from one transgression resulting in condemnation (Romans 5:16).

Jesus said while telling of Himself:

"He that believeth on Him [Jesus] is not condemned; but he that believeth not is condemned already, because he hath not believed in the name of the only begotten Son of God" (John 3:18, KJV).

Also Paul declared in Ephesians 2:3 that the Christians to whom he was writing formerly had been *by nature* the children of wrath.

Regardless of parents, church membership, country of birth, or religion—everybody already is a member of the kingdom of darkness. Whatever your church affiliation, you will find this doctrine of original sin in your church's tenets of faith. Perhaps it is not preached and taught very often—but it is there.

Is There No Hope for the Human Race?

Oh, yes, there's hope. Jesus was Himself the solution to the problem of original sin when He came to earth to die for all sinners.

For God so loved the world, that He gave His only begotten Son, that whoever believes in Him shall not perish, but have eternal life (John 3:16).

In 1 John 5:19 we read, "We know that we [Christians] are of God, and the whole world lies in the power of the evil wicked one."

Christians are people who also were born into Satan's kingdom but were transferred out of that kingdom of darkness into the kingdom of God's dear Son Jesus when they accepted Him as Saviour and Lord. Their citizenship has been transferred!

And we Christians have the key to the problem of original sin—which is causing all this evil on earth today. Ours should be an *offensive* stance. We do not have to leave people trapped and doomed in Satan's evil kingdom. We must wage an offensive war against Satan for the souls of lost people.

Jesus' reason for coming to earth was to die on the cross to rescue those who are in Satan's kingdom. When He went back to heaven, He left us to finish the job by inviting those lost ones to believe in Jesus and be transferred out of their captivity. His Word calls us to "go into all the world and preach the gospel to all creation" (Mark 15:15).

So evangelism is not a project, an assignment, or just a method of church growth. It is all-out war for the souls of the subjects already in the kingdom of darkness. And every week on planet Earth a million more souls are born into that kingdom of darkness!

THE OFFENSIVE AND DEFENSIVE BATTLE

In all warfare there are two opposite tactics—offensive and defensive. The side of the defense is desperately trying to hold onto its own territory and citizens, while the offense is trying to push ahead, taking territory and people captive for its own.

In the spiritual world the two rulers also are waging two completely different kinds of war for people. One is defensive and one is offensive.

Satan, surprisingly, is on the *defense* in the battle for souls. Although he certainly is on the offense against those already Christians, Satan's battle *for* souls is just the opposite. *Since he already owns them before they accept Jesus as Saviour, he is trying desperately to hold on to those who are his.* Satan is battling to hold on to what he won in the Garden of Eden.

But in the battle for souls, Jesus and His followers definitely are on the *offense*—actively going after the citizens of Satan's kingdom.

(The defensive role of Christians, of course, is necessary against Satan's personal attack on us as he shoots his fiery darts and prowls about as a roaring lion to see which of the Christians he can devour. He keeps us too busy defending ourselves and too exhausted putting out his fires to wage our offensive war against him.)

Jesus' parting words as He left earth for heaven called His followers to wage this *offensive war* for converts, rescuing them from the kingdom of darkness. While Satan can sit back feeling smug about all those billions already captive in his kingdom of darkness, Christians cannot do that. We must work to get the citizens of that kingdom transferred to Jesus' kingdom.

Our marching orders are in Jesus' great commission:

> "Go therefore and make disciples of all the nations, baptizing them in the name of the Father and the Son and the Holy Spirit, teaching them to observe all that I commanded you" (Matthew 28:19-20).

When Jesus appeared to Paul (formerly Saul) on the Damascus road, He told him why He was calling him. Jesus was not calling Paul to take a defensive stance and be protected from Satan when he became a Christian. No, Jesus forcefully sent Paul into an offensive battle for the people in Satan's kingdom. Jesus said:

> For this purpose I have appeared to you, to appoint you a minister and a witness . . . to open their eyes so that they may turn from darkness to light and from the *dominion of Satan to God* (Acts 26:16-18, italics added).

Our job, with Paul, is to rescue those Jesus said were condemned already.

NEW AGE MOVEMENT

Where does the New Age movement fit into this kingdom warfare? Why is this spiritual movement sweeping America?

Because an unusually huge spiritual void has sprung up recently. People have discovered that materialism, intellectual advancement, scientific prowess, and even Godless communism—so widely touted as the answer to all human problems—have not turned out to be solutions.

On a long transcontinental flight our intelligent, meticulously groomed stewardess finished her duties and sat down in an empty seat near me. She whipped out a book and announced loudly to the person sitting next to her that she finally had found the answers to life in that book.

Soon all eyes were fastened on her as she extolled the virtues of the new religion she had found in Shirley MacLaine's book, *Dancing in the Light*. People started asking questions, revealing that they too needed answers for their lives. Excitement mounted and voices rose to a higher and higher pitch as she waved the book triumphantly in the air—and my heart started to ache! The answer for those "condemned already" isn't in pagan beliefs of communicating with spiritual entities thousands of years old and reincarnation modernized and Americanized.

After all our material, intellectual, and political advancement, people are groping even more than ever for something spiritual to fill the deep void. And the New Agers are rushing in, capitalizing on this thirst for spiritual reality.

Shockingly, New Age leaders are getting and passing on actual answers from real spiritual beings. The problem is that these answers are from the kingdom of darkness, not from God's kingdom of light.

TODAY'S CONFUSION

Today there are many widespread beliefs that work like opiates in our society to dull our spiritual senses. They keep us lulled from seeing the truth of the two kingdoms.

There is a subtle, almost creeping *universalism* that is insidiously taking over the thinking of many Christian churches. It is that pie-in-the-sky philosophy that everybody is OK and will be OK in the afterlife. We are lulled to sleep in an "I'm OK and you're OK" society, ignoring the fact that without

Jesus they are not OK—but condemned.

Then there is a vague, largely unspoken belief in a vast, undefined *never-never land between the two kingdoms* with most people floating freely in it. The border of this neutral land just sort of blends into the kingdom of evil on one side or the kingdom of good on the other. Most people believe in those two extremes, but they feel the ordinary "doing-the-best-I-can" people don't belong in either of them.

My secretary told me she had just heard a sermon where the pastor explained that many in his audience still were *sitting on a fence,* trying to decide which leader to follow—Jesus or Satan. Not true. Those in his congregation who had not accepted Jesus already belonged to Satan. So the only decision they could make was to leave that kingdom of darkness and be transferred into Jesus' kingdom. Nobody is sitting on a fence trying to decide *which* spiritual ruler to follow—because there is no fence.

Then there are those who readily accept the concept of heaven, but refuse to believe Jesus was telling the truth when He spent more time talking about hell than about heaven. They believe God is too loving to send anybody to eternal punishment.

A pastor's wife defiantly said to me, "Don't give me that Satan stuff. I have a God of love!" Well, I do too. But my God loved enough to send His only begotten Son to wage war on the enemy who captured humanity in the Garden of Eden—Satan!

These deceptions are straight out of the kingdom of darkness—from the leader Satan, certainly not from the Bible. But they have been extremely effective in undermining our battle for the lost—in our families, neighborhoods, and around the world.

Through the centuries religious thought has been changed by silver-tongued orators, flaming zealots, or poignant-penned intellectuals. Today we have added seminars, tapes, and videos along with radio and television personalities—all trumping their brand of truth or heresy. But this kind of recent confusion is different. It has come unannounced, quietly taking one little piece of our thinking at a time. It seems so harmless, so logical, almost evolutionary. It appears to be just the natural progressive flow of thoughts as we humans think we are discovering more and more "truth." But actually, it is a gradual take-over of our minds and our society with the lie that started in the Garden of Eden.

Early in the 1970s my prayer group and I attended a meeting in a church to check out a speaker who claimed to have paranormal power. It turned out to be very occult, including automatic writing. But we were stunned when the pastor closed the meeting in prayer thanking God for this wonderful new "truth" we had the privilege of learning.

There seems to be no intelligent being behind this deluded thinking. But is there? Oh yes! It is the carefully devised and successfully masterminded scheme—in the spirit world—by the head of one of the kingdoms, Satan! A scheme to keep all his subjects captive in his evil kingdom.

But we Christians have the answer to Satan, the Prince of Darkness: Jesus!

TWO
THE PRINCE OF THE
KINGDOM OF DARKNESS
Ephesians 6:11-12

I n order to be effective warriors in this spiritual battle
for Satan's captives, we need to understand the rulers of
the two spiritual kingdoms—their power, their tactics,
and their ultimate ends.

First, let's take a look at Satan, the Prince of Darkness,
ruling his kingdom with the host of demons he commands.

IS SATAN REALLY REAL?

Are those without Jesus being held captive in the kingdom of
an *actual being*?

Are you skeptical? Do you wonder if Martin Luther was
deluded, or even deranged, when he threw an inkwell at the
devil? Or if Jesus was—when at His temptation He said,
"Begone, Satan!" (Matthew 4:10).

The Bible clearly describes the Christian's enemy in this
spiritual warfare raging on earth.

Put on the full armor of God, that you may be able to
stand firm against the schemes of the devil. For our struggle is not against flesh and blood, but against the rulers,
against the powers, against the world forces of this darkness, against the spiritual forces of wickedness in the heavenly places (Ephesians 6:11-12).

In 1972, with that early occult explosion popping up everywhere, I decided I needed to be more informed, so I enrolled in the "Theology of Satan" course at a local seminary. Our class sat stunned as the professor gave us our first big assignment: "Go find a live one—and write up your findings." Live *what*? "Someone on whom Satan and his demons have an unusual grip," he explained.

Many of us questioned how we ever could do such an assignment. But, to our amazement, everyone of us did find a "live" one. In fact, without my even looking for them, God gave me two people caught in Satan's clutches. One was a recent convert who had fourteen witches in her immediate family. And since she had been two years old, they had practiced their witchcraft rituals on her. She came to me for help while I was speaking in her city, telling me that after a pastor had delivered her from demons a couple weeks before, the void left in the pit of her stomach felt like a big hole. Questioning whether this was real and actually could happen, I asked my professor. He solemnly nodded and replied, "You've found your live one, Evelyn."

The other was a deaconness of a large evangelical church who had been born into a pagan Eastern religion and thought she had accepted Jesus several years before—but was not rid of all the evil beings still occupying her body. It was after midnight in the big empty meeting hall of a California mountain retreat center. Most of the lights had been turned out as those being counseled had trickled back to their bunks. All except this lady who had struggled for hours after our meeting trying to get rid of whatever had been bothering her so insidiously all those years.

Alone with her in her deep distress, and completely naive as to what was happening, I held her in my arms while she identified, confessed, and denounced sin after sin. But with each one she denounced, she wretched and expelled long strings of gross matter from her nose. When the gruesome experience was finished, she trembled and then smiled with relief—and the two of us left that eerie scene to make our way through the blackness of night to our beds. But the next morning, beaming radiantly, she thanked me profusely for her new life in Jesus!

This time I raced up to my theology professor, spewing out all the gory details of my encounter, I gasped, "What was *that?* Have you ever heard of . . . ?" He looked steadily at me and answered, "Yes, that was demons, Evelyn."

I went a little numb as my mind flashed back to that eerie midnight scene—my complete calm, absence of fear, and feeling only compassion for her. Reacting like any mother would, helping a vomiting little child. Stunned, I knew I had met Satan's kingdom head-on!

Our seminary professor had taught that theology subject for years, but when I enrolled he was fresh from a speaking tour in Ethiopia—where he had found some "live ones." Being warned by the missionaries that he might encounter some peculiar activity during his preaching about Jesus, he asked what he should do if it happened. "Oh, you'll know," they said confidently. But he was totally unprepared for the woman sitting right in front of him suddenly being lifted from her seat and being propelled in mid-air to the back of the room. Needless to say, we had a very experientially convinced professor that semester. He, and I, knew Satan was real!

The whole world lies in the power of the evil *one* (1 John 5:19, italics added).

My close friend Kathryn Grant also knows Satan is real. We were roommates as our group left the International Prayer Assembly in Seoul, Korea, to visit China in 1984. While many in our group had felt the evil that seemed to descend on us as we entered that country with its history of anti-God government, we were not prepared for the terror Kathryn experienced our first night there.

The day's events had set the stage, as she had been shocked at the reality of the filth and poverty of the communists commune produced by a pagan regime. It brought back vivid memories of the first time she visited a pagan shrine as a young new missionary in Japan and was overcome by the terrifying presence of evil she sensed. She had become violently sick to her stomach as she watched human beings actually bowing to and kissing ugly demon-inhabited gods, carved with their own hands.

Suddenly in the middle of the night Kathryn began to whisper from her bed, "Evelyn, Satan is in this room. Pray, Evelyn, pray!"

Kathryn was not one given to dreams or hallucinations. After her missionary service, she had gone on to be a top executive in two large Christian organizations. That night in China Satan really was there.

Later, asking her to describe what Satan was like, she replied, "It was a black presence, like a tall human but no facial features. Definitely occupying space—the space on the right side of my bed, toward my feet. All around my bed was a black mist like a rectangular wall with clean cut edges. But in my bed there was light. Satan was standing in the black mist.

"There was no fear that he would attack me," she continued. "Just the horror of his presence. It was the same horror I had the first time I went to a pagan temple in Japan." She brightened as she said, "But when we prayed, it faded."

However, as we both lay in our beds continuing to pray, Kathryn suddenly said, "Evelyn, he's coming again!" Again there was no fear—just the misery of his presence. And again our prayers sent him disappearing out of our room. Satan is very real!

PERSON OR EVIL INFLUENCE?

Do people actually belong to a *being* before they accept Jesus as their Saviour, or are they just under an *evil influence*?

The Bible is very clear that Satan is not some nebulous evil influence floating around which settles on people, but is an actual being. He talked, acted, and traveled while tempting Jesus on the Mount of Temptation (Matthew 4:3-5). God talked to Satan after our first parents sinned (Genesis 3:14). God also carried on a two-way conversation with Satan about Job.

If you believe the Bible, you must believe Satan is a person. In Ephesians 6:11-12 we are told that we stand against the schemes of *the* devil, struggle against *the* rulers, against *the* powers, against *the* world forces of this darkness, against *the* spiritual forces of wickedness in the heavenly places. These are unseen supernatural beings. We Christians are struggling against the leader and members of an organized evil spirit world.

In James 4:7 Christians are told how to handle the devil, and then how he will respond: "Resist *the* devil, and *he* will flee from you (italics added)." No mere *influence* ever could flee from us when we battle him—only a *being*.

Jesus told the Jewish leaders that they were of their father the devil (John 8:44). "Satan," a proper noun, entered into Judas (Luke 22:3) resulting in his betraying Jesus and then committing suicide (Acts 1:18). Satan thwarted Paul from going where he desired (1 Thessalonians 2:18), and some young widows turned aside and followed Satan (1 Timothy 5:15).

Paul said in 2 Thessalonians 3:3, "But the Lord is faithful, and He will strengthen and protect you from *the* evil one" (italics added).

Only a being can be called by actual names. Some of the Bible's names for Satan are: evil one, god of this age, prince of the power of the air, ruler of this world, serpent, dragon, accuser, tempter, deceiver, murderer, liar, sinner, Beelzebub, ruler of demons, roaring lion, and devil.

It is a mistake to omit one of the letters of the primary name of Satan and spell it *e-v-i-l* instead of *d-e-v-i-l*.

A committee member for one of my prayer seminars in a large California city discovered first hand that Satan was a real being and not an evil influence.

Since 1980 we have averaged approximately 25 percent of all our seminar audiences praying audibly to accept Jesus or make sure He really is their Saviour and Lord. We actually have had several times where 50 percent, 75 percent, and once even 80 percent prayed that prayer. Of course, this mass transferring of souls from Satan's kingdom to Jesus' has made

Satan very unhappy. And we have experienced some unusual and powerful attempts by Satan to hinder them.

One Friday evening in the spring of 1989 my interdenominational local committee gathered for the usual praying for the next day's seminar. But it didn't turn out to be an ordinary prayer meeting. During our praying, one of the things I prayed was my usual "Father, deliver us from the evil one tomorrow." Then, addressing that evil one, Satan, I commanded him—in the name of Jesus and in the power of the blood Jesus shed on the cross—to let go of tomorrow's participants who he was still deceiving into believing they were Christians when they really were not. Then I asked God to cleanse that sanctuary with the blood of Jesus of all evil thoughts, words, and actions that had taken place there. Next I told Satan in the name of Jesus to leave.

Suddenly a committee member started to cry, sobbing off and on through the prayer meeting. When it was over, she admitted to the committee why she had been such an ineffective member. Although she was the president of a large area-wide women's organization, she told us why she had done so little work for the seminar. "My church doesn't ever talk about Satan," she said. "In fact, I didn't know he really existed. But right after I signed up to work for this seminar, a voice . . . ." She hesitated, and added, "I've never heard a 'voice' in my whole life. I didn't know what it was. But 'it' told me not to bother with this seminar as it would be a failure, nobody would come, and nothing would happen. It said not to waste my time on it. So, that's why I didn't do anything." Pausing as if to grasp the significance of what she was about to say, she gasped, "I actually was obeying that voice!"

She sobbed softly before she could continue. "When Evelyn was telling Satan to get out of our seminar, suddenly something in me just popped. And, it was gone! The negative feelings, the oppression I had felt these six months—disappeared." An incredulous look crossed her face. In shock she said, "I know now that voice was Satan!"

Needless to say, the rest of us were in shock also. But the

next day we understood the significance of that spiritual battle. The audience was very large in spite of Satan's prediction. And when I asked how many were not sure they really knew Jesus as their personal Saviour and Lord, two-thirds of them prayed out loud making sure! They were transferred from Satan's kingdom to the kingdom of God's dear Son, Jesus—in spite of Satan's efforts. No wonder he went to such extreme ends to hinder that seminar!

Your adversary, the devil, prowls about like a roaring lion, seeking someone to devour (1 Peter 5:8).

JESUS KNEW SATAN AS A PERSON

Jesus recognized "evil" as a person all through His earthly ministry. He knew from the beginning it was a person from whom He must rescue fallen humanity.

The Son of God appeared for this purpose, that He might destroy *the works of the devil* (1 John 3:8, italics added).

In 25 of the 29 passages in the New Testament referring to Satan, Jesus is speaking.

Jesus called Satan by name, even calling him "the ruler of the world" in John 14:30 and 16:11. And in His temptation He interacted with Satan as a person (Matthew 4:1-11). If Jesus had not been tempted by a being, the temptation would have had to have come from within Himself, an impossibility since Jesus was sinless. Or, worse yet, He would have had to be mentally deranged, conversing with an "influence".

In recognizing Satan and demons as beings, Jesus could not have been just accommodating Himself to the superstitions of that age, for He, being God, was omniscient, knowing all things. When Jesus called Himself "the truth," He ruled out any lying or yielding to erroneous thinking of the day.

Much misunderstanding about whether Satan is a person or an influence has come from how Jesus' Lord's Prayer was translated. Until recently in most Bibles Matthew 6:13 was written "deliver us from *evil*." But what Jesus actually said was a proper noun, the name of someone: "Deliver us from the evil *one*."

When Jesus went back to heaven, He left His followers to be witnesses in order to win those still in Satan's kingdom to Himself. But He knew they would be battling the supernatural war without Himself there personally to help them. So He prayed in His high priestly prayer for the Father to deliver them from the evil one—a being, not an influence.

I do not ask Thee to take them out of the world, but to keep them from the evil *one* (John 17:15, italics added).

Jesus also interacted with Satan's demons as personalities. He talked to them, cast them out, and had complete power over them at all times. They recognized Jesus and called Him the Son of God. "What do *we* have to do with You, Son of God? Have You come to torment *us* before the time?" (Matthew 8:29, italics added)

There was no doubt in Jesus' mind that demons and their master Satan were real—and that the spiritual battle over souls would be with him.

TODAY IN AMERICA

Most Christians don't have trouble believing the Bible's coverage of Satan and his demons "way back then in Bible times." And it has been easy through the years for Christians to accept that Satan is active in "heathen countries." They readily gasp at missionaries' slides of witchcraft and Satanic rituals in a "foreign land."

Up until now most Americans have never seen Satan in his raw form. Missionaries are more sensitive to Satan because they have fought him so long. But suddenly Satan has come out of the closet in America, and we aren't at all sure what to do about it. Some laugh at it, some ignore it, some try to explain it away theologically, while others believe God couldn't possibly allow it in this 20th century.

However, Satan worship and demonic activity in the United States have exploded in our faces in the last twenty years. And the life into which the ruler of the kingdom of darkness is leading some of his subjects is despicible beyond words, defying all that is good, pure, and honest.

On September 27, 1987, our Minneapolis "Star Tribune" newspaper reported seminars being held to train police investigators to recognize signs of satanic motives behind bizarre and inexplicable crimes such as: frenzied devil worshipers in black robes sacrificing animals and sometimes people before candle-lit altars, ritual sacrifices, child molestation, grave robberies, teen suicides, mutilated goats, pentagrams, burning candles, satanic graffiti, and homicides committed by people dabbling in Satanism through the demonic lyrics of some heavy-metal rock bands. These seminars were necessary because most police don't even know this exists, some won't believe it, and many don't want to get involved.

My husband and I sat riveted in shock recently watching a TV special on Satanism. The people actually involved told their own stories on the program. Horror stories like a young woman telling how she murdered her mother, stepfather, and a store clerk as a sacrifice to prove allegiance to Satan and hatred toward society. Kids told of killing other kids in the name of Satan and drinking victims' blood. Teenagers reported their involvement in grave robbing and making necklaces out of right little finger bones. Then the high priest of the Satanist Church in San Francisco made a brief appearance and claimed most active Satan worshipers are professional and business people—and even in our military. His daughter shocked us with how widespread this worldwide religion really is.

The national newcasters screamed "Tabloid reporting!" but, though shocking and difficult for all of us to accept or even watch, everything was extremely well documented. Credible law enforcement and investigative witnesses joined the present and former Satan worshipers.

Our newspapers and newcasts continuously shock us with stories of the "Texas Massacre," Satan-worshiping murderers such as Charles Manson, grave robbings, and mutilated animal and sometimes human bodies being discovered. A hideous reality in our country has come to light these past few years. We are horrified—but act as if we are helpless to stop it.

These are the end results of the control of the Prince of the Kingdom of Darkness out of which we are commanded by Jesus to rescue unbelievers.

PERCENTAGE OF INVOLVEMENT

However, most people still in Satan's kingdom are not even aware of the hideous lifestyle of those actually in Satanic worship who have sold out to him. And the majority will never become involved in it.

But they belong to the same Satan. No matter how upright, cultured, educated, and successful they are, they nevertheless are members of the same evil kingdom of Satan until they accept Jesus. The only difference is the percentage of involvement in the evil lifestyle of the Prince of Darkness.

Amazingly, most Christians seem ignorant of the kingdom out of which they were transferred when they accepted Jesus. And many don't even know they were by birth members of Satan's Kingdom.

But, much more serious, is that such a large percentage of Christians are oblivious of the evil kingdom their unsaved family members and acquaintances still are in—no matter how moral their lifestyle may seem.

SAME SATAN FOR CHRISTIANS TOO

You may be shocked as a Christian to realize this Satan who instigates these atrocities *is the same Satan who gets us to serve him*—to whatever extent he can. Every time we yield to his temptation to lust, hate, lie, or commit any other sin, it is that same Satan who encourages and propagates it. Satan introduced and is responsible for all sin in believers and nonbelievers alike.

It is the same Satan who, disguising himself as an angel of light (2 Corinthians 11:14), fools us into believing that "it can't be sin if it fulfills our needs," who fools our children into believing the Satanic rock and roll is just "modern music," who deceives our teens into believing "suicide is a good and honorable way out of problems."

It is the same Satan who plants pride through our successes, discouragement or even despondency through our failures, our apathy toward a lost world, divisions in our churches, and our prayerlessness.

After Jesus ascended back to heaven, He wrote to His churches on earth through the Apostle John and warned about the amazing amount of Satan's shocking activity in His church. These activities are still going on in Christ's church today, but frequently are not recognized by preacher or parishioner. Satan is working hard to get—not only those already in his kingdom—but us Christians, to serve him in a deeper and deeper way. (See Revelations 2 and 3.)

NEW AGE MOVEMENT

Even the New Age Movement with its self-proclaimed beneficial results, is another kind of activity within Satan's kingdom.

Its spirit guides communicating the New Age "Gospel" through channelers to awestruck followers, and believing reincarnation (being born over and over to try again) are just two of the evidences that its followers are desperately seeking a satisfying spiritual reality. But instead of finding biblical new life in Jesus, they are getting advice from the evil spirit world, and have become involved in the doctrine *of* demons explained in 1 Timothy 4:1.

> But the Spirit explicitly says that in later times some will fall away from the faith, paying attention to deceitful spirits and doctrines *of* demons (italics added).

Most New Age followers sign up quite innocent of the source of the power in the movement, and they are ignorant of which supernatural kingdom they will be operating in and who their leader actually is. And they are completely ignorant of how diabolical that leader really is. Everything seems so positive—so new—so chic. And so harmless!

How Did This Start on Earth?

How did Satan get all people born on earth into his kingdom?

Why did Jesus consistently call Satan "the *ruler* of this world?" (See John 12:31, 14:30, 16:11). Why did Paul call him "the *god* of this world" in 2 Corinthians 4:3-4? Why, according to 1 John 5:19, does "the whole world lie in the power of the evil one?"

Didn't God declare in Genesis 1:31 that everything was "very good" after He created it? So, what happened?

God had given Adam and Eve control over earth. "Then God said, 'Let Us make man in Our image, according to Our likeness; and let them rule over . . . all the earth'" (Genesis 1:26).

But when Adam and Eve sinned by obeying Satan's advice rather than God's, they were cast out of the Garden of Eden by God, and lost that control. Chapter three of Genesis tells us how they broke their relationship with God by sinning. (Paul validates this Old Testament account in 2 Corinthians 11:3 referring to the serpent deceiving Eve.)

And their sinning passed on their sin and their condemnation to all humans:

> So then as through one transgression there resulted condemnation to all men. For as through the one man's disobedience the many were made sinners (Romans 5:18-19).

And the world had fallen into the hands of the instigator of that sin—Satan. When Satan tempted Jesus on the Mount, he led Jesus up and showed Him all the kingdoms of the world in a moment of time. And the devil said a very shocking thing to Jesus:

> I will give You all this domain and its glory; *for it has been handed over to me,* and I give it to whomever I wish. There-

fore if You worship before me, it shall all be Yours (Luke 4:6-7, italics added).

WHERE DID EVIL COME FROM?

How did Satan get to be evil in the first place to tempt Adam and Eve?

Wasn't he created as Lucifer, the wisest and most beautiful angel, occupying a place of authority and privilege in heaven? Doesn't Jude 9 say he is more powerful than the archangel Michael? Yes, all these things are true according to the description accepted by Biblical scholars as that of Lucifer in Ezekiel 28:11-19:

> You were blameless in your ways from the day you were created, until unrighteousness was found in you . . . And you sinned. . . . Therefore I have cast you as profane from the mountain of God. . . . I cast you to the ground (28:15-17).

Sin appeared in the perfect, holy environment of heaven when Lucifer became proud and wanted to become like the most high God—and be worshiped by all. But no sin can stay there, so God cast Satan out of heaven.

But, amazingly, God threw him not into hell—which was prepared for him—but to earth.

> How you have fallen from heaven, O star of the morning, son of the dawn! You have been cut down to the earth (Isaiah 14:12).

In August 1969, I was sitting at a cottage window high on a bluff on the shore of Lake Michigan witnessing the blackest, most violent storm we had seen in fifteen years. The lightning was violently tearing apart the sky and cracking into the angry lake. The next morning as I sat on that storm-washed beach reading my Bible, I read these words of Jesus: "I was watching Satan fall from heaven like lightning" (Luke 10:18).

The picture was still so vivid in my mind, I almost felt I

too had seen Satan splitting open the sky and crashing to earth. But why earth? If I had been God, I would have cast him straight to hell!

RULING REALMS

But Satan does not operate nor rule from hell now. He will be punished there, but that is in the future. His place of operation according to Ephesians 6:12 is "in the heavenly places." This is the sphere around planet Earth where the spiritual battle is raging today.

The "heavenly places" is not "heaven." Heaven is the place of abode of the Father, the only true God. It is the place of absolute authority in the universe. Jesus voluntarily came *from* heaven (John 6:38), and it is the place to which God raised Christ after His earthly mission was completed (1 Peter 3:22). That's why Satan was expelled from heaven when he sinned. Only God rules from heaven!

That's why Jesus taught us in the Lord's prayer to direct our prayers, not to beings in the heavenlies, but to *the Father* in heaven. (Matthew 6:9) The communicating with beings by the New Agers, occult followers, and Satanic worshipers is with those spirits in the heavenlies, not heaven.

SATAN—A DEFEATED RULER

Jesus came to earth for only one reason. It was not so we could have a Christmas manger scene, Christmas angels, the star of Bethlehem, or Easter morning. No. Again, it is 1 John 3:8:

The Son of God appeared for this purpose, that *He might destroy the works of the devil* (italics added).

And defeat him, Jesus did. Satan is already defeated—and he knows it!

That through death He [Jesus] might render powerless him who had the power of death, that is, the devil (Hebrews 2:14).

However, Satan did *cause* the incarnation of Jesus. How? By introducing sin onto earth. And God said "without shedding of blood there is no forgiveness" (Hebrews 9:22). So Christ came to shed His blood on the cross to provide forgiveness for the sin that Satan caused.

When Jesus appeared publicly for His earthly ministry, John the Baptist saw Him coming, and declared, "Behold, the lamb of God who takes away the sin of the world!" (John 1:29)

And He Himself [Jesus] is the propitiation for our sins; and not for ours only, but also for those of the whole world (1 John 2:2).

Jesus paid the price on the cross and became the payment for the sins of those Satan won in the Garden of Eden.

But Satan's doom was sealed long before Calvary. He was cursed by God immediately after causing the fall of humanity into sin through Adam and Eve.

And the Lord God said to the serpent, "Because you have done this, cursed are you" (Genesis 3:14).

Jesus' incarnation and death was the fulfillment of God's words to the serpent, the devil, in Genesis 3:15 after Satan deceived Eve and she ate: "And I will put enmity between you and the woman, and between your seed and her seed; He shall bruise you on the head, and you shall bruise Him on the heel." And it happened.

Peter, preaching on the day of Pentecost said, "Jesus the Nazarene . . . delivered up by the predetermined plan and foreknowledge of God, you nailed to a cross by the hands of godless men and put Him to death. And God raised Him up again, putting an end to the agony of death since it was impossible for Him to be held in its power" (Acts 2:22-24). Death was defeated through Jesus' death!

Philippians 2:9-11 tells us what happened after Jesus' death on the cross:

Therefore also God highly exalted Him, and bestowed on Him the name which is above every name, that at the name of Jesus every knee [including Satan and his demons] should bow, of those who are in heaven, and on earth, and under the earth, and that every tongue should confess that Jesus Christ is Lord, to the glory of God the Father.

Defeated unequivocally!

SATAN'S PRESENT STATUS

Satan, although powerful, is being allowed by God to operate on earth only temporarily and according to God's rules.

Satan's power is limited by *God's permissive will.* Since Satan was cursed and doomed by God in the Garden of Eden, God has allowed Satan to have power on planet Earth—but it definitely is limited power. As a being created by God, everything Satan does must be allowed by the sovereign God, the creator.

Satan is limited by the *extent of power* God chooses to let him use. Satan is not omnipotent—only God is. Satan is not the opposite of God—one being a "good god" and the other being an "evil god." No, Satan is only a fallen angel.

Satan also is limited by *human will.* God made all humans free moral agents. We have the right to choose to be transferred out of Satan's kingdom by accepting Jesus as Saviour. And once we belong to Jesus, Satan can only tempt us—not make us fall.

Satan is limited by *time.* He knows his time is limited before he will be cast into hell. His demons too know their time to harass people on earth will come to an end. The ones possessing the Gadarenes recognized Jesus and cried out to Him, "What do we have to do with You, Son of God? Have You come here to torment us *before the time?*" (Matthew 8:29, italics added)

Satan is on a time schedule, and he knows it. Could this be the reason for the frenzied flurry of satanic and demonic activity today?

SATAN'S END

The Bible closes with the ultimate outcome of both rulers, Satan and Jesus. The place, conditions, and how long are clearly spelled out. Revelation 20:10 emphatically states:

> And the devil who deceived them was thrown into the lake of fire and brimstone, where the beast and the false prophet are also; and they will be tormented day and night forever and ever.

Satan will be not only *defeated* for eternity—but *punished* for eternity!

The sin and suffering Satan brought to earth will boomerang on himself and his cohorts, the demons. The torment that he introduced to humanity will be what he will experience forever and ever!

I have almost worn out 1 John 4:4 in my battle with Satan, confidently defeating him over and over with its fabulous declaration:

> Greater is He who is in you [Jesus] than he [Satan] who is in the world!

I sing it, I whisper it, I shout it—because it's true. I know!

THREE
THE RULER OF THE KINGDOM OF LIGHT
John 8:12

In soul-winning, we need to understand not only the ruler *from* whose kingdom people are being rescued at salvation but, more importantly, the Ruler *into* whose kingdom they are being transferred—Jesus.

Who is this Jesus, the ruler of the kingdom of light?

Are Jesus and Satan co-contenders for the final spiritual victory? Are they equal rulers of equal spiritual kingdoms? Are they battling to see which ruler is going to win the spiritual superbowl or world series of the universe?

Jesus contrasted Himself with the kingdom of darkness by announcing: "I am the light of the world; he who follows Me shall not walk in the darkness, but shall have the light of life" (John 8:12).

Why should we be eager to get people transferred out of Satan's kingdom into Jesus' kingdom?

How foolish it is for us to invite a non-believer to Jesus without being absolutely sure which of the rulers of these kingdoms is victor—and knowing that we are bettering their spiritual status.

It would seem that Satan had the upper hand when he caused the incarnation of Jesus. The sin he brought to planet Earth was the reason Jesus left heaven to die so those sins could be forgiven (Hebrews 9:22). It certainly appeared Satan was in control when he actually could take Jesus to the pinnacle of the temple and a high mountain while tempting Him (Matthew 4:5 and 8). Jesus' agony in the Garden of Gethsemane, when He sweat drops like blood, was a high price to pay for. the sin Satan introduced to earth (Luke 22:44). Then Satan must have felt like the winner when those who captured Jesus mocked and blasphemed Him, spat on Him, and scourged Him until blood ran down His back. How smug Satan must have felt when they stripped Jesus, put a scarlet robe on Him, and pressed a cruel crown of thorns into His brow (Matthew 27:26-31).

Then when the mob cried out, "Crucify Him! Crucify Him!" and Jesus died that agonizing death on the cross, Satan surely must have thought he was the stronger of the two spiritual rulers—and had won the spiritual war of the ages, killing the leader of the opposing kingdom.

But just the opposite was true.

VICTORY ON THE CROSS
Here is what *really* happened when Jesus died on that cross—and the effects it had on those needing to be transferred from Satan's kingdom into Jesus' kingdom.

Jesus paid the price for all *sin* Satan brought to earth—once for all on the cross. Those who accept Jesus have all the state of sin into which they were born erased from them by the blood of Jesus.

Jesus Christ . . . who . . . released us from our sins by His blood (Revelation 1:5).

Romans 5:19 gives us the answer to people's original *condemnation* Satan caused: Jesus! Although born condemned already, those who accept Jesus are at that time made righteous.

For as through one man's [Adam's] disobedience the many were made sinners, even so through the obedience of the One [Jesus] the many will be made righteous.

The greatest promise possible for those formerly *alienated* and *hostile* in mind and *engaging in evil deeds* is in Colossians 1:21-22:

> Yet He [Jesus] has now reconciled you in His fleshly body through death in order to present you before Him holy and blameless and beyond reproach.

A lovely Christian lady in Durban, South Africa, came to me after I had taught how terrorists in Northern Ireland had found Christ in prison because so many people prayed for them. She agonized as she confided, "I *can't* pray for those terrorists in our country." Searching my face and noting my surprise, she continued, "But—what should I pray?"

My answer was so simple, "For them to find Jesus, of course. Then they won't be terrorists any more!"

Paul showed us in Colossians 2:13-15 what happened to both the new believer and Satan's hierarchy through the cross:

> And when you were dead in your transgressions and the uncircumcision of your flesh, He made you alive together with Him, having forgiven us all our transgressions, having canceled out the certificate of debt consisting of decrees against us and which was hostile to us; and He has taken it out of the way, having nailed it to the cross. When He had disarmed the rulers and authorities, He made a public display of them, having triumphed over them through Him.

When I checked with the campus pastor of a fine Christian college in the midwest to see if there was a need for this book before I wrote it, he answered an emphatic, "Yes." Then he cautioned, "But be sure you start at the cross, Evelyn. As I teach our college students to share Jesus, I tell them they have to understand the cross before they can be effective witnesses. They must have a firm grasp on the fact that Jesus defeated Satan, sin, evil, and death on the cross once and for

all—before they are ready to win others to Jesus."
Also Satan was stripped of his power over death.

That through death He [Jesus] might render powerless
him who had the power of death, that is, the devil (Hebrews 2:14).

The whole battle between Jesus and Satan is summed up in
Philippians 2:8-11 with Jesus' stunning victory.

And being found in appearance as a man, He [Jesus] humbled Himself by becoming obedient to the point of death,
even death on a cross. Therefore, also God highly exalted
Him, and bestowed on Him the name which is above
every name, that at the name of Jesus *every* knee should
bow, of those who are in heaven, and on earth, and under
the earth, and that *every* tongue should confess that Jesus
Christ is Lord, to the glory of God the Father (italics
added).

When Jesus gave up His spirit on the cross, it was not the
execution of a helpless victim. No, incredible supernatural
miracles rocked the area when Jesus died. The veil of the
temple was torn in two—supernaturally—from top to bot-
tom. Then an earthquake shook the earth and split the rocks,
terrifying the city when the tombs flew open. Many bodies of
the saints who had fallen asleep were raised, coming out of
the tombs and entering the holy city—appearing to many.
When the centurian, and those who were with him guard-
ing Jesus, saw the earthquake and the things that were happening, they became very frightened and said, "Truly this
was the Son of God!" (Matthew 27:51-54)
Jesus appeared on earth specifically to destroy the works of
the devil (1 John 3:8); and when Jesus, hanging on the cross,
cried, "It is finished"—it *was* finished!
Jesus was completely victorious over Satan on the cross of
Calvary. There are no future re-matches. No best two out of
three tries. It was a final, complete victory for Jesus.

This is the finished work of Jesus on the cross we offer to those who are still captive in the kingdom of darkness.

JESUS' BEGINNING VERSUS SATAN'S

We need to know the difference between Satan and Jesus before we invite people out of Satan's kingdom and into Jesus'. Where did they both come from? How did each get his start?

First, Satan is a created being. But Jesus has always existed! Jesus is, and always has been, *God*. John starts his Gospel by telling us that:

In the beginning was the Word [Jesus], and the Word was with God, and the Word *was God* (John 1:1-2, italics added).

And Jesus created all things—even Satan.

For by Him all things were created, both in the heavens and on earth, visible and invisible, whether thrones or dominions or rulers or authorities—all things have been created by Him and for Him (Colossians 1:16).

PRE-EXISTENT DEITY

What price was Jesus willing to pay for the lost ones you are trying to win to Him? How important can you tell them they are to Jesus?

Tell them He was the only pre-existent baby ever born on planet Earth—in spite of the pagan belief in reincarnation in foreign countries and now rampant in America.

Tell them before He came to earth, Jesus lived in the perfect environment of heaven with the Father. It is a holy abode with no pain, sorrow, or sin. (That's why Satan could not stay there when he sinned.)

But, amazingly, Jesus was willing to leave that environment and power temporarily—to redeem those you are introducing to Jesus from the sin Satan caused. He willingly came and dwelt among *us*—fallen creatures with sickness, dirt, poverty, violence, and decaying bodies. For us and for them.

Jesus was willing to come to a planet made by Himself—planet Earth. And He was willing to put Himself, pre-existent deity, through nine months inside one of the human bodies He created! He allowed Himself to be bumped along over the dusty roads inside His earthly mother—so she could be taxed in Bethlehem—and He could be born where God's Word had predicted. He even put Himself through the very humbling birth process in a birth canal full of human bacteria and germs.

He was willing to be born in an animal stable with no sterilization, no bed linen, the dust of 70 miles of traveling sticking to His mother, no deodorant sprays, no showers!

Then He willingly lived for thirty-three years subject to all the miseries of this earth, and died by one of the cruelest methods of torture—crucifixion.

But death and the tomb could not hold Him, and He burst forth that first Easter morning.

It was just forty days later that Jesus ascended back to that perfect environment—victorious over Satan, the one who made His temporary absence necessary by introducing sin to planet Earth.

WHEN DID JESUS BECOME LORD?

Do you, consciously or subconsciously, have a time in Jesus' life when you feel Jesus became—or will become—Lord?

Are you waiting for Jesus to return triumphantly to earth in the clouds of the sky to become Lord? Or are you vaguely waiting for Revelation 19:16 to come to pass: "And on His robe and on His thigh He has a name written, King of Kings and Lord of Lords"?

You probably agree Jesus was Lord when Stephen, while being martyred, "gazed intently into heaven and saw the glory of God, and Jesus standing at the right hand of God." But do you believe Jesus became Lord *only* when He got back to heaven after His incarnation and ascension away from planet Earth?

Or do you feel it was on the cross when He defeated Satan

that Jesus became Lord? Or when the grave could not hold Him, and He arose from the dead that first Easter morning? It certainly was at Jesus' resurrection the full significance of the title "Lord" became understood. It was then the women found the stone rolled away and, entering, they did not find the body of the *Lord* Jesus (Luke 24:3). But was that when Jesus *became* Lord?

No, Jesus was Lord during His earthly ministry—before His death and resurrection. As Lord, He had total power over Satan's works on earth—sin, sickness, and unclean spirits. Typical were those of the great throng from all Judea and Jerusalem and the coastal region of Tyre and Sidon. People "who were troubled with unclean spirits were being cured. And all the multitude were trying to touch Him, for power was coming from Him and healing them all" (Luke 6:18-19).

Also during Jesus' earthly ministry, the demons of Satan's kingdom always recognized Jesus, knew who He was, talked with Him, submitted to His authority and power over them, and unequivocally obeyed Jesus at all times. And Jesus always was Lord over them, silencing them and casting them out.

And demons also were coming out of many, crying out and saying, "You are the Son of God!" And rebuking them, He would not allow them to speak, because they knew Him to be the Christ (Luke 4:41).

Actually, before His earthly ministry even started, Jesus already claimed to be Lord. At His temptation by Satan, He emphatically told Satan, "It is written, you shall not tempt the *Lord* thy God."

Do you feel it is possible Jesus was Lord while He was in Mary's womb? He was! Elizabeth asked the pregnant Mary, "And how has it happened to me, that the mother of my *Lord* should come to me?" And the angels announced to the shepherds on the Judean hills that the tiny new-born baby in Bethlehem was "Christ the *Lord*" (Luke 2:11).

But did Jesus have to come to earth to become Lord? No.

Jesus always has been Lord. Peter preached on the day of Pentecost:

> Therefore let all the house of Israel know for certain that God has made Him *both* Lord and Christ—this Jesus whom you crucified (Acts 2:36, italics added).

Was Peter referring to some event in Jesus' life that entitled Him to become Lord in addition to their Messiah? No. Jesus has been Lord from the beginning. He not only created all things, but was *before* all things. He always has been the image of the invisible God (See Colossians 1:15-17).

When Satan aspired to be like God, he was cast from heaven. Satan has *never* been—nor ever will be lord. But Jesus *always* has been—and always will be—Lord.

FALSE TWENTIETH CENTURY "JESUS"

Today there still are people wanting to be lord—and claiming to be Jesus. Someone said there are six hundred in California alone.

But our Jesus of Nazareth is the one God claimed was His beloved Son both at Jesus' baptism and on the Mount of Transfiguration. Also our Jesus is the only one the demons recognize as the Son of God, crying out: "What do we have to do with You, Jesus of Nazareth? Have you come to destroy us? I know who You are—the Holy One of God!" (Mark 1:24)

The London meeting hall they engaged for my last seminar there, to our horror, was also being used for meetings by a man from India claiming to be Jesus. (He said he could travel anywhere on earth without transportation—but had arrived in London's Heathrow Airport on an intercontinental jet!) I cringed as I had to lay my notes on the same pulpit, and struggled with an evil permeating the very room and inhibiting my freedom to speak. But it was prayer—in the name of the *real* Jesus—that finally broke that evil power. And God mightily moved through the day's seminar. Jesus warned about this prior to His second coming:

Then if anyone says to you, "Behold, here is the Christ," or "There he is," do not believe him. For false Christs and false prophets will arise and will show great signs and wonders, so as to mislead, if possible, even the elect (Matthew 24:23-24).

Even though they still are trying, none of Satan's followers ever will be the *Lord Jesus* either!

TWENTIETH CENTURY JESUS

But who is the Jesus of this last decade of the twentieth century? Who is the Jesus you are inviting people to accept as Saviour and Lord?

Is He still the babe of Bethlehem, just the Good Shepherd, the one who did not open His mouth before His accusers? Is He only the Lamb being led to the slaughter? Is He still being crucified on the cross? Is He even just the Christ who rose from the dead whom His followers saw for forty days? Or just the Jesus they saw leave planet earth at His ascension in the clouds?

Are you still trying to introduce unbelievers only to the babe in a manger or a sacrificial Lamb on the cross?

Who is the Jesus of *today*? He is the Jesus with all these earthly events completed—sitting at the right hand of God the Father in heaven. He is the Jesus the Apostle John saw at the end of the first century A.D.—and who commanded John to write down His description in Revelation chapter one so we would know.

Is He the Jesus of *Now* to you? Is He the one John saw?

The seminar committee at the Royal Air Force Base in Upper Heyford, England, had been praying together two years for my 1989 prayer seminar there. When I joined them the night before, we gathered together to pray around a huge oval shaped table. Soon we all became acutely aware of an unusual fulfilling of Jesus' promise in Matthew 18:20 that "where two or three have gathered together in My name, there I am in their midst." Many wiped tears, some wept, one sobbed openly at the powerful sense of Jesus' presence.

But it wasn't the babe of Bethlehem, or even the risen Lord I saw as I too wept. Seemingly towering above us as we bowed low before Him was the Jesus the Apostle John saw. It was the powerful, ruling commander in chief—with His robe reaching to His feet, a golden girdle across His breast, His head and hair white like wool, like snow. And His eyes were like a flame of fire, His feet like burnished bronze when it has been caused to glow in a furnace. His voice was like the sound of many waters. In His right hand He held seven stars, the angels or messengers of the seven churches. And His face was like the sun shining in its strength. (See Revelation 1:12-16.) This is the Jesus John saw!

I stopped to weep once again as I wrote this last paragraph. My Jesus!

The Apostle John's reaction to seeing Jesus as He is now was, "I fell at His feet as a dead man." But Jesus laid His right hand on the terrified John and said, "Do not be afraid; I am the First and the Last, and the living One; and I was dead, and behold, I am alive forevermore, and I have the keys of death and of Hades" (Revelation 1:17-18).

There was much apprehension among my family and my board about my going to South Africa two years ago. Clashing of whites with blacks, blacks with blacks, coloreds with blacks, and coloreds with whites was rampant. Reports of "necklacings" among competing black tribes were filtering to America—where a gasoline filled automobile tire was placed around the victim's body and lit, taking twenty minutes to kill him or her. Just before leaving, I read those words of Jesus to John. I wept as I too saw Jesus. Then I prayed, "Oh, Jesus, would You—could You—even lay Your hand on *me*?" Through the weeks there, when things were physically and humanly impossible, or danger loomed menacingly near, over and over I stopped—and felt my Jesus' hand on me. Sustaining me. Protecting me. My Jesus!

The people needing to be transferred out of Satan's kingdom need to see the Jesus of now. Have we ourselves lost the wonder of who Jesus is? Have we lost the awe of leading people to *our Jesus*?

RULING REALMS

Where do we tell those being transferred out of Satan's kingdom their new Lord is right now?

Where Jesus has been since His ascension until this 20th century is clearly stated in the Bible. After recording Jesus' Great Commission, Mark 16:16 says Jesus was received up into heaven, and sat down at the right hand of God.

Satan, in contrast, rules from the locale of "the heavenlies," that sphere around planet Earth.

Peter wrote to tell us where Jesus is now. He is at the right hand of God, having gone *into heaven* after angels and authorities and powers had been subjected to Him (see 1 Peter 3:22). Jesus has been installed as the God of the Universe!

Saul (Paul) on the Damascus road at midday saw a light *from heaven* brighter than the sun shining all around him. And when he and those journeying with him had fallen to the ground, a voice spoke to Saul. When Saul questioned who was speaking, the voice replied, "I am Jesus whom you are persecuting."

Don't play games with this Jesus, such as pretending you are sitting on His lap. No, He is sitting on the right hand of the Father in the throne room Isaiah saw with the seraphim crying one to the other, "Holy, holy, holy!" (Isaiah 6)

But heaven isn't just the abode of Jesus. The difference is more than mere locality. Heaven is the place from which He rules. From heaven He has absolute headship over all angelic and human rule, authority, power, and dominion.

These are in accordance with the working of the strength of His [the Father's] might which He brought about in Christ, when He raised Him from the dead, and seated Him at His right hand in the heavenly places far above all rule and authority and power and dominion, and every name that is named, not only in this age, but also in the one to come. And He [the Father] put all things in subjection under His [Jesus'] feet, and gave Him as head over all things to the church, which is His body, the fullness of Him who fills all in all (Ephesians 1:19-23).

A group of one hundred of us left the first International Prayer Assembly in Seoul, Korea and took a trip through Hong Kong into China. The very real sense of the evil in a country whose government is anti-God descended like a heavy cloud when we passed the border into that country. While visiting a huge, then empty hall used by that government, all of us stood overwhelmed in a little knot on the main floor, looking up at the vastness representing the greatness of that earthly kingdom. Then someone suggested we "test the acoustics." And we all sang at the top of our lungs the chorus based on Philippians 2:9-11:

"He is Lord, He is Lord.
He is risen from the dead, and He is Lord.
Every knee shall bow, every tongue confess,
That Jesus Christ is Lord!"

Heaven also is the place from which our Lord and Saviour will come back to earth the second time. At Jesus' ascension, these were the hopeful words uttered to His followers:

Men of Galilee, why do you stand looking into the sky? This Jesus, who has been taken up from you into heaven, will come again in just the same way as you have watched Him go into heaven (Acts 1:11).

How exciting to be able to tell those we are reaching for Jesus that He is coming back—to solve all the problems on planet Earth. And they will be able to reign with Him.

Paul told the Christians at Philippi that our citizenship is in heaven from which we eagerly wait for a Saviour, the Lord Jesus Christ to come back, He then will transform our present bodies into conformity with the body of His glory. And He will do it by exerting the power that He has to subject all things to Himself. (See Philippians 3:20-21.)

And, of course, the most thrilling promise for those we are inviting to accept Jesus is the place of their final abode. It is not being recycled back to earth to try again. It is not being condemned to oblivion. It is being together with their Jesus—in heaven forever and ever.

Two Opposites

The two rulers of the spiritual kingdoms are personally as opposite as is possible to be in our universe. They are diametrically opposed as to what they are trying to accomplish in the spiritual warfare. Those who come to Jesus need to know how different their old and new rulers really are.

While one, Satan, is evil personified—the Other, Jesus, is holiness personified. While Satan is engaged in offensive spiritual battle against Christians so they won't win his subjects out of his evil kingdom, Jesus is engaged in offensive spiritual battle to rescue those He loves and died for out of that evil kingdom. The one ruler, Satan, defensively is trying to keep all those born into his kingdom in that kingdom, while the Other, Jesus, weeps with compassion for all those captive in the kingdom of darkness.

What the two rulers brought to earth is amazingly different with opposite motives and opposite outcomes. Jesus came to bring reconciliation, peace, and holiness while Satan brought alienation, hostility, and evil deeds (Colossians 1:20-21). Satan brought death (Genesis 3:19), and Jesus brought life (Ephesians 2:5). While we were yet sinners, Christ died for us—while Satan, when humans were still innocent and sinless as created, brought sin and death (see Romans 5:8).

Satan is perpetuating the reincarnation lie that physical death on earth is not final, while the Bible clearly says in Hebrews 9:27, "It is appointed for men to die *once* and after this comes judgment." But Jesus put an end to the agony of death for those who believe on Him (Acts 2:24). They will meet Him as Saviour, while those still in Satan's kingdom will meet Him as judge.

The evil ruler, Satan, is the created; Jesus is the creator. Satan is a fallen angel; Jesus the image of the invisible God (Colossians 1:15). Satan lost the battle of the cross; Jesus won. Satan is limited in his power; Jesus has all authority in the universe. Two absolutely opposite rulers—Jesus and Satan!

JESUS' LAST VERBAL COMMUNICATION WITH US

Jesus must have wanted to make sure we on earth knew what He is like in this current biblical time era, for in the last verbal communication we have from Jesus He dictated His own description of Himself. Giving each church a piece of His description, here is a composite picture of the reigning, ruling Lord:

"The One who holds the seven stars (the angels of the churches) in His right and walks among the seven golden lampstands (the churches). "The first and the last, who was dead and has come to life." "The One who has the sharp two-edged sword." "The Son of God who has eyes like a flame of fire, and His feet are like burnished bronze." "He who has the seven Spirits of God and the seven stars." "He who is holy, who is true, who has the key of David, who opens and no one will shut, and who shuts and no one opens." "The Amen, the faithful and true Witness, the Beginning and the creation of God" (Revelation 2 and 3).

This is the Jesus up to now in our twentieth century!

FINAL OUTCOME

Rescuing a soul out of Satan's captivity rescues him or her from the *loser's* kingdom.

The contrast of the final ends of the two rulers is almost incomprehensible to our human finite minds. Satan will be cast into hell to be punished eternally; Jesus will reign forever and ever and ever!

Revelation 19:11-16 burns into our hearts the glorious, victorious culmination of this age with our Jesus reigning:

And I saw heaven opened; and behold, a white horse, and He who sat upon it is called faithful and True; and in righteousness He judges and wages war. And His eyes are a flame of fire, and upon His head are many diadems; and He has a name written upon Him which no one knows except Himself. And He is clothed with a robe dipped in blood; and His name is called The Word of God. And the armies which are in heaven, clothed in fine linen, white and clean, were following Him on white horses. And from His mouth comes a sharp sword, so that with it He may smite the nations; and He will rule them with a rod of iron; and He treads the winepress of the fierce wrath of God, the Almighty. And on His robe and on His thigh He has a name written, *King of Kings, and Lord of Lords.*

Those we win to Jesus will meet Him, not as their judge—but as their King of Kings and Lord of Lords!

Two opposite rulers—but certainly not equal rulers! In the spiritual battle of the universe Satan always has been the loser, and Jesus always has been the winner.

And those we win to Jesus are not only rescued from the doomed kingdom of the Prince of Darkness—but are citizens of the kingdom of Jesus. Eternal winners!

FOUR
WHY BOTHER
TO FIGHT?
Matthew 10:28

W hy bother to spend time and effort getting people transferred from one spiritual kingdom to another? Because the consequences are so terrifying. Everyone who isn't rescued from Satan's kingdom (into which they were born) will spend eternity, not with Jesus in heaven, but with Satan in hell.

IN HELL?
The Bible and Jesus use the word that almost has been deleted from our Christian vocabulary in recent years: "hell." Today it is basically used as a swear word, not a horrible place of punishment.

In order to get serious about winning souls, perhaps we need to get a new grasp of the final destiny of those still in the kingdom of the Prince of Darkness. Why don't (or won't) we handle one of Jesus' main teachings any more? Are we too sophisticated? Are we too uncomfortable to face it?

Of the twelve times the word "hell" (Greek: Gehenna) is used in the New Testament, eleven of them are by Jesus Himself.

> And do not fear those who kill the body, but are unable to kill the soul; but rather fear Him who is able to destroy both soul and body in hell (Matthew 10:28).

Jesus made sure His followers knew clearly what hell is. Explaining the parable of the tares sown by the devil, Jesus said that the Son of Man will send His angels to separate the wicked from the righteous—and cast them into the *furnace of fire*. Then Jesus looked gravely at His followers and asked them, "Have *you* understood all these things?" (Matthew 13:51, italics added).

Is Jesus asking the same question of *us* today? Have *we* understood hell?

Jesus treated hell as a definite, *inescapable* place. Reprimanding the religious leaders of His day for being full of hypocrisy and lawlessness while outwardly trying to appear righteous to people, Jesus blasted at them with these words of the certainty of hell: "You serpents, you brood of vipers, how shall you *escape* the sentence of hell?" (Matthew 23:33, italics added)

"WHAT'S SO BAD ABOUT HELL?

This is a question you might be asking. Some people actually believe hell is just an extension of the fast lane lifestyle here on earth—with intensified strob lights, sensuous hard rock music, gyrating enticing bodies, unending lustful orgies. Isn't it uninhibited satisfying of all sinful appetites—without the bothersome influence of religious fanatics?

Oh, no. According to Jesus hell is a place of *fire*. Unquenchable, eternal fire. He repeatedly referred to hell as fire. In Matthew 13:49-50 Jesus warned:

So it will be at the end of the age; the angels shall come forth and take out the wicked from among the righteous and will cast them into the furnace of fire.

And this is not just a nice fire at which to warm our toes on a cold night. No. It is a place of *torment*. Jesus concluded Matthew 13:49-50 with this awesome description of what they will be doing—not winking with provocative lips and leering sensuous grins, but "there shall be weeping and gnashing of teeth."

Hell also is a place of *punishment*. It is not intended by God as a deterrent or a place of reformation, but a place of punishment.

Dealing out *retribution* to those who do not know God and to those who do not obey the Gospel of our Lord Jesus (2 Thessalonians 1:8, italics added).

Hell is the vindication of a holy God. Holiness is God's ruling attribute. So hell, as well as the cross, indicates God's estimate of sin.

Hell is *banishment*. It is being banished from all good influence of God and the society of righteous people.

And these will pay the penalty of eternal destruction, away from the presence of the Lord and from the glory of His power (2 Thessalonians 1:9).

Speaking of entering the kingdom of heaven, Jesus in Matthew 7:23 said of those who practice lawlessness, "Then I will declare to them, 'I never knew you; *depart from Me*'" (italics added). Eternal separation alone will make hell almost unbearable.

Jesus explained hell's *duration*, using such words as "eternal" and "everlasting." In Mark 9:44 He said, "To go into hell, into the unquenchable fire." And then adds, "Where their worm does not die, and the fire is not quenched" (9:48.) If heaven is eternal, hell must be too, because Jesus used the same word to describe the suffering of the wicked and the happiness of the righteous in Matthew 25:46.

The end of those who worship the beast and his image, and receive his mark on their foreheads or hands is foretold in Revelation 14:10-11:

He also will drink of the wine of the wrath of God, which is mixed in full strength in the cup of His anger; and he will be tormented with fire and brimstone in the presence of the holy angels and . . . the Lamb. And the smoke of their torment goes up *forever and ever*; and they have no rest day and night (italics added).

Jesus shocked His followers by telling them that if a part of their body caused them to stumble, they were to pluck out the eye, cut off the hand or foot. For, He said, it is better to go through *life* (here on earth) with one eye or crippled or lame, than to be cast into *eternal* hell. (See Matthew 18:7, 9.)

OCCUPANTS OF HELL

Who will be in hell? Jesus in Matthew 25:41 clearly gives us the two categories of beings who will be cast into the eternal fire: (1) the devil and his angels for whom hell was specifically prepared (with the beast and the false prophet), and (2) the accursed ones (people).

As the Bible comes to a close in the Book of Revelation, we read these terrifying words: "And the devil who deceived them was thrown into the *lake of fire and brimstone*, where the beast and the false prophet are also; and they will be tormented day and night forever and ever" (Revelation 20:10, italics added).

But Satan will not be alone in hell. This punishment will include all angels who fell with Satan and were cast out of heaven into hell and committed to pits of darkness, reserved for judgment. (See 2 Peter 2:4.) There is no salvation provided for angels who fell. Also Jude 6 says, "And angels who did not keep their own domain, but abandoned their proper abode, He has kept in eternal bonds under darkness for the judgment of the great day."

All the demons will be in hell—and they know it. When Jesus confronted the demons possessing the violent Gadarene, He cast them out and they entered a herd of swine. But before being cast out by Jesus, they had cried, "What do we have to do with You, Son of God? Have You come here to torment us *before the time?*" (Matthew 8:29)

However, much more devastating to us is that hell is also for people.

A woman at the European Council of the Protestant

Women of the Chapel in Germany last month came to me after I had said lost people would be in hell. She said, *"We* don't believe there will be people in hell—only Satan and his demons."

"What does the Bible say?" I questioned her. "It is the final authority on all doctrinal questions."

But for the cowardly and unbelieving and abominable and murderers and immoral persons and sorcerers and idolaters and all liars, their part will be in the lake that burns with fire and brimstone, which is the second death (Revelation 21:8).

After this terrifying announcement, John then gives the breathtakingly fantastic description of the Holy City, the New Jerusalem: having the glory of God . . . brilliance like a very costly crystal-clear jasper . . . angels at the twelve gates . . . walls of jasper . . . streets of pure gold like transparent glass . . . the Lord God and the Lamb its temple . . . no need of the sun or moon, for the glory of God illumined it and its lamp was the Lamb . . . and no night there . . . (verses 11-25).

But John follows it in verse 27 with: "And nothing unclean and no one who practices abomination and lying shall ever come into it, but only those whose names are written in the Lamb's book of life!"

It is into "eternal fire" prepared for the devil and his angels that Jesus will send accursed people.

And if anyone's name was not found written in the book of life, he was thrown into the lake of fire (Revelation 20:15, italics added.)

Since being transferred out of Satan's kingdom into Jesus' kingdom is the only way humans can escape this horrible eternity, is it puzzling to you that we Christians don't engage actively in this spiritual battle for the soul of our loved ones, colleagues, neighbors, Sunday School pupils, Bible study students, and the lost around the world?

My heart breaks every time I think of *all* human beings who do not believe on Jesus during their lifetime being cast into eternal punishment with the devil and his fallen angels. All those not rescued from Satan's kingdom—*by us!*

WHEN *THEY* DON'T WANT TO BE BOTHERED

Perhaps you are asking, why should we bother people about their spending eternity in hell—when they don't want to be bothered? Why disturb them when they are perfectly content where they are spiritually? It may be their apathy, ignorance of the reality of eternal punishment, or even a deliberate choice of that life after death rather than heaven—but they certainly are not bothering *themselves* with their eternal destiny!

But Jesus bothered even when they didn't want a Saviour. He left His perfect environment in heaven and paid the price on the cross so that they could be rescued from hell. "While we were yet sinners, Christ died for us." And "we shall be saved from the wrath of God through Him" (Romans 5:8-9).

Jesus bothered because He knew there would come a time when they all *will* bow before Him. A time when at the name of Jesus every knee shall bow, of those who are in heaven, and on earth, and under the earth. (See Philippians 2:10.) If not as their Lord, as their judge.

In John 3:36 Jesus makes very clear the position of people who don't bother to be bothered. "He who believes in the Son has eternal life; but he who does not obey the Son shall not see life; but the *wrath of God* abides on him."

WHY DON'T *WE* BOTHER?

There are many different reasons, better called excuses, why we don't bother to tell the lost about Jesus.

1. We think it isn't nice to be pushy. This is one of Satan's most effective lies today in keeping Christians from sharing

Jesus with the lost. Most Christians feel it is much better to be "liked" than to push our Jesus on somebody.

2. *We are afraid to be called intolerant.* Being tolerant of everybody's beliefs seems to be the "in" thing these days. We have confused accepting them as persons of worth with accepting what they believe.

3. *We are ashamed of Jesus.* Many affluent Christians are ashamed of their Jesus because He was not socially, financially, or academically in the same class as those they should be winning to Him. Jesus does not fit with those they are trying to impress—or climb their social, financial, or corporate ladder.

4. *We feel embarrassed.* It is not as hard to talk to strangers, especially those we know we will never see again, about Jesus as it is to those we know well. It can be embarrassing to admit to colleagues, family members, and friends that we are different than they are. And it is especially embarrassing to share that we think we have something better than they have—Jesus.

5. *We see evangelism as just "a project."* We largely have reduced soul-winning to evangelistic projects. In our churches, and sometimes in our parachurch organizations, we are given quotas, questionnaires, and assignments. These we complete—sometimes grudgingly, but frequently sincerely—even with zeal. However, the real reason for winning those persons to Jesus just isn't there—to rescue them from their captivity in Satan's kingdom of darkness.

6. *We are ignorant of Jesus' basic doctrine.* What Jesus really came to teach has lost popularity in our preaching and teaching in recent years, resulting in woefully ignorant Christians. His theme of "repent or die" has been replaced with plans, programs, and projects. The uncomfortable doctrines of the Bible have been obscured or lost in "topics" and "electives."

7. *We're too busy to bother.* Of course, the only reason some of us have for not witnessing is that we are too busy. We are completely absorbed in the tyranny of the urgent of trying to make ends meet, hold our families—or our own lives— together. We have no time or energy left for other people.

8. We are deluded that hell is on earth. Many Christians these days are confusing "hell on earth" for the real thing. They tend to think of a bad marriage, intolerable working conditions, or abuse from children or other people as "hell on earth." And they actually feel it is all the hell God will mete out.

9. We say, "Not me!" One of the reasons we don't bother, is that subconsciously, or even consciously, we don't think Jesus meant *us* when He gave His Great Commission. When He said to go make disciples of all nations, He meant pastors, evangelists, or missionaries—and those with a special calling to witness to the lost.

10. We don't understand their hurting—especially when they cloak it in three piece suits or fashionable clothes, hair, and nails. Their deep needs are missed by us because of a stoic "I'm fine" expression—which crumbles in their solitude.

11. We don't accept our responsibility. It hasn't crossed the minds of many Christians that if *they* don't tell them of Jesus, perhaps nobody will. And they will be eternally doomed to everlasting torment.

12. We don't care.

ARE WE REALLY CHRIST-LIKE?

Most Christians really want to be Christ-like, but we have formed a picture of Jesus in our minds made up of preconceived ideas which fit *us*, not necessarily *Him*. We have a vague idea that our description of Jesus is biblical—without ever studying the Bible to find what He really was like.

Some character and personality traits we are prone to leave out are: Jesus' anger at sin, His unequivocal denouncement of those not believing in Him, His narrow-mindedness about ways to get to heaven, His strict rules about being righteous here on earth, His intolerant view of other religions that exclude Himself. We tend to overlook His sacrificial lifestyle, His giving His own life for the lost, His compassion for those eternally doomed, His weeping over them, and His longing to gather them to Himself.

If we really were like Jesus we would *bother* to reach out to those dying eternally in their sin—as He did.

CONTRASTING MOTIVATION FOR BOTHERING

The rulers of the two supernatural kingdoms have opposite reasons for *bothering* to wage spiritual warfare.

Jesus bothered to come to earth and die—*to set the captives free.* (See Luke 4:18.) And He said of Himself in John 8:36, "If therefore the Son shall make you free, you shall be free indeed." *Satan,* in contrast, bothers to fight this spiritual battle to keep people captive in his evil kingdom, eternally doomed.

God the Father's reason for bothering is incredible—*His love.* In John 3:16 Jesus explained God sending Him to die on earth: because He *loved the world so much.* God was willing to give His most precious possession, His only Son, to die to defeat Satan. Satan, on the other hand, rebelled against this loving God and, knowing he is doomed eternally, is determined to take as much of mankind as possible with him to his eternal punishment.

God bothered to redeem mankind because He is not willing that any should perish but "desires all men to be saved," (1 Timothy 2:4); while Satan spends full time feverishly battling to keep those in his kingdom doomed until they die—and it is too late to be rescued from perishing in hell.

Satan is the Father of Lies, and his all-encompassing motivation is to dupe humans into believing his lies about "evil is good and good is evil," "everybody is OK," "reincarnation," etc. But Jesus bothered to come to bring the *truth,* refuting the deception of the father of lies, Satan.

One of Satan's main current lies is reincarnation. He is trying to negate our concern at being judged in the future for our current lives—by convincing people that they can try again and again. But reincarnation, the New Age lie that people can be born physically over and over again, is refuted unequivocally in the Bible in Hebrews 9:27: "It is appointed for men to die *once,* and after this comes *judgment.*"

Satan knows his end, and he wants to take as many people as possible to eternal torment with him. Jesus also knows His own end, and longs to have us all reign in paradise with Him—eternally!

The diametrically opposed motivations of the two spiritual leaders is appalling: love vs. destruction, truth vs. lies, freedom vs. captivity, God's acceptance vs. His wrath, life vs. death!

WHY BOTHER?

Because Jesus said it matters desperately whether or not we bother: "And these will go away into eternal punishment, but the righteousness into eternal life" (Matthew 25:46).

All human beings who do not believe on Jesus during their lifetime will be cast into eternal punishment with the devil and his fallen angels. All those not rescued from Satan's kingdom—by us!

But all whom we do bother to rescue will shine forth as the sun in the kingdom of their Father.

> The harvest is the end of the age; and the reapers are angels. Therefore just as the tares are gathered up and burned with fire, so shall it be at the end of the age. The Son of Man will send forth His angels, and they will gather out of His kingdom all stumbling blocks and those who commit lawlessness, and will cast them into the furnace of fire; in that place there shall be weeping and gnashing of teeth. Then the righteous will shine forth as the sun in the kingdom of their Father (Matthew 13:39-43).

Why bother? Because it makes a difference. A life and death difference!

The most powerful tool Satan has in the battle for souls is: getting Christians not to bother. It's all he needs to win—by default!

FIVE
GOD'S ARMOR ON FOR VICTORY
Ephesians 6:10-20

T he Prince of Darkness fights a fierce, unethical, and diabolical battle for souls. Being the father of lies, Satan's tactics are underhanded and deceitful. He operates under none of the rules we expect among human leaders. He has no honor or integrity to defend.

No human tactics ever could outsmart his cunning guises. No human defenses could withstand his supernatural ruthless onslought without divine help.

God knows all this. He understood Satan completely before He called us into the battle for souls against him. God has clashed with Satan since his rebellion against God in heaven, and is thoroughly aware of his diabolical ways.

So God doesn't expect Christians to try to rescue souls out of Satan's kingdom of darkness without supernatural help. God knows exactly what kind of protection, wisdom, and power we will need in this exasperating and fiendish battle.

Consequently, God provided supernatural strength, armor, and weapons for His soldiers.

Finally, be strong *in the Lord,* and in the strength of *His* might. Put on the full armor of God, that you may be able to stand firm against the schemes of the devil (Ephesians 6:10-11, italics added).

GOD'S SPIRITUAL ARMOR

However, putting on God's armor does not mean passively waiting for God to pre-fit a suit of protective clothing up in heaven—and then wrapping it around us as it drops from the sky. Nor is God's armor a suit of custom-tailored clothes furnished by the master Tailor up there—and all we have to do is reach up, grab it, and drape it around around ourselves.

No, "putting it on" means the believer takes the initiative and deliberately does something with that armor, piece by piece. Although God's armor is furnished by Him, it actually requires personally appropriating moment by moment the armor's truth, righteousness, peace, faith, salvation, and the Word of God.

God's armor is available from Him to all Christians. Our part is to be spiritually disciplined enough to *put on, take up,* and *use* all of this armor so that we will be able to stand and withstand the schemes of the devil in the spiritual battle here on earth.

And it is these *actions* that will produce a *lifestyle*—the lifestyle which contains the secret of being able to stand against the schemes of the devil.

Therefore, *take up* the full armor of God, that you may be able to resist in the evil day, and having *done* everything, to stand firm (Ephesians 6:13, italics added).

This armor and the rulers of the kingdoms at war are described in Ephesians 6:10-20.

NOT AUTOMATIC PROTECTION

There are Christians who feel the Bible's 1 John 4:4 promise of "Greater is He who is in you [Jesus] than he that is in the world [Satan]" is their *automatic* insulation against any victories of the devil without their doing anything. And many believe when Jesus came to live in them at salvation, which He did, their battle with Satan ceased. But just the opposite is true. Paul wrote the warning about putting on the armor of God to "saints"—those already having Jesus living in them. (See Ephesians 1:1.)

In fact, the battle with Satan only *starts* when we become Christians. Before that, we are members of Satan's domain of darkness—and certainly are not at war with him. The call to put on armor is the Christians' summons to prepare for conflict—a war that has been raging since the Garden of Eden.

When we Christians enter the battle to rescue souls, we automatically escalate Satan's attacks on us. As long as we don't threaten his kingdom, he doesn't worry too much about us. But when we obey Jesus and get into the battle for souls, we must strengthen our defensive stance against Satan and be strong in the Lord. This is why God provided armor for us.

Billy Graham, having been used by God in the release of more captives from Satan's kingdom than perhaps any other person on earth today, understands this battle and its solution. In a TV interview with David Frost reported in the Minneapolis Star Tribune July 10, 1989, Mr. Graham said he often receives death threats but pays no attention to them. "I have no bodyguards. . . . They [frequent death threats] are just put aside. I feel like I'm clothed in the armor of God, and I'll go on as long as God wants me to."

Are you thinking, "Since Satan is not omnipresent, if he is busy attacking Billy Graham, I'm safe?" True, Satan cannot be at all places at one time as God can, but he has his whole host of demons, all the rulers, powers, forces of darkness, and wickedness under his command. He is the mastermind of the whole spiritual battle which has been going on since the Garden of Eden on earth, and he is in full control of those evil beings in his huge hierarchy.

> For our struggle is not against flesh and blood, but against the rulers, against the powers, against the world forces of this darkness, against the spiritual forces of wickedness in the heavenly places (Ephesians 6:12).

We need God's armor because our battle is not against flesh and blood. Our human know-how, wisdom, and strength never can equip us for this diabolical spiritual battle.

STANDING AND WITHSTANDING

Amazingly, Ephesians 6 gives no mention of Christians falling or not being able to stand. The rulers, powers, world forces of this darkness, and the spiritual forces of wickedness described in verse twelve already are defeated by Jesus—and they know it.

But there is a clear-cut condition for our being able to stand and withstand—by making full use of the spiritual armor God provides.

When we become actively engaged in the spiritual battle for souls, Satan will aim his attack at any missing parts of our armor he can spot. God did not promise us to be able to stand without a truthful, righteous, peaceful, full-of-faith lifestyle—using our salvation and the Word of God to its fullest.

This standing and withstanding is a *defensive stance* against the evil forces. It must be there *before* we dare to launch our *offensive* efforts against Satan for lost souls. There is no way to keep from falling if our "standing firm" is not there first.

"THE DEVIL MADE ME DO IT"

This is a convenient cop-out for Christians, but this is not true. Satan cannot *make* us fall he can only *tempt* us to fall. All human beings have free wills, and make choices as to whether to yield or to put on their armor and resist Satan's fiery darts.

Although God has provided all the armor we ever will need to defend ourselves against Satan's attacks, we must use it all. Putting on the whole armor of God will equip us to resist and successfully stand against the subtle and open attacks of the Prince of Darkness.

WHEN WILL WE NEED THE ARMOR?

Ephesians 6:13 tells us it is in *the evil day* we will need to be sure we are equipped for the battle with evil. But when will that time come?

It certainly seems that "evil days" are upon us. As I returned to America from training the Protestant Women of the the Chapel of the U.S. European Military Command last month, I received a phone call from their past president. After praising God for how the week had gone, she became very somber and changed the subject. "Evelyn," she said, "I've been gone with the military six years, and I didn't come home to the same country that I left. All the drugs, child abuse, abortions, rape, pornography, lack of morals in society, schools, our government! *I don't even recognize my country any more!*"

These days truly are evil, so we need to put God's armor on *now*. When the attacks come, it may be too late to get this whole lifestyle in place.

FULL ARMOR

We do not have a choice as to which piece or pieces of God's armor we will put on. Both times the word "armor" is used in the Ephesians 6 passage, the word "full" describes it. Why? Every soldier knows wearing *almost all* of his protective gear will not guarantee his safety. So, if one item of our spiritual armor is left off, the enemy will be able to defeat us at that spot.

> Put on the *full* armor of God. . . . Therefore, take up the *full* armor of God (Ephesians 6:11, 13, italics added).

THE DEFENSIVE PIECES OF ARMOR

There are five pieces of defensive armor we put on to protect ourselves.

1. Truth. The *first* piece of our armor we are to take up and put on is *truth*.

> Stand firm therefore, having girded your loins with truth (Ephesians 6:14).

This is not *the* truth, which would be the true message of the Gospel, but just "truth." This is the truthfulness, reality, and sincerity of character of the regenerate Christian.

Also, it is more than just *believing* truth. Putting on truth means *living* truth every moment of every day. Jesus said in

John 3:21: "But he who *practices* the truth comes to the light, that his *deeds* may be manifested as having been wrought in God" (italics added).

A young man from our former pastorate was finishing a doctoral program in one of our country's leading seminaries, and I asked him, "What are they talking about in the coffee shop these days, John?" (I knew their informal conversations are good indicators of the direction our future church leaders are going.)

"They are discussing," he replied, "whether it is enough to preach the truth, or do they have to live it too." Then he quoted one future pastor as saying, "I'll preach the truth— but my personal life is my own business."

No, God's Word says there is no way that young preacher will be able to stand in this evil day unless he "girds up his loins with truth." In Paul's day having the loins girded meant the Romans soldier was ready for active duty. So putting on truth today is an absolute necessity in being ready for active duty in the spiritual battle.

While writing this book, I have begged God many, many times to keep me from saying or even intimating anything that was not absolute and complete truth. As I have listened to advice given to me by Christians leaders for this book, I have cringed as one says this and another says that. "Oh God," I have cried over and over again, "show me YOUR truth!"

At a committee meeting of outstanding Christian leaders recently, the conversation drifted to this book I'm writing. "Make sure it is theologically accurate, Ev," one cautioned— while the others chimed in their agreement. As I nodded, my eyes were panning the group. My heart was bursting to ask, "*Whose* theology?" I knew they themselves were divided on at least a couple of doctrines absolutely essential to this book. I tightened the resolve deep within me. "Only truth, Lord. Only YOUR truth!"

But where do you find *truth?* In God's Word, the Bible. Working with people of all denominations for twenty years in my prayer ministry has kept me in *only* what the Bible teaches about prayer. Using actual Scripture, not what I—or they—think, has worked. We really have not had a problem in all these years.

One of our main reasons for not having truth is that we have not spent enough *honest* time in the Scriptures. We all have our preconceived theological ideas and have a tendency to fit what we read and study in the Bible into them—instead of the other way around as it should be.

After teaching a point on "hell" at a recent retreat, someone said again, "We don't believe there will be people in hell."

My answer? "Do you believe the Bible?"

"Yes."

"Well, Jesus said in Matthew 25:41 that He will say to those accursed ones (people) on His left to depart into the eternal fire which has been prepared for the devil and his angels. And the Bible also says that if anyone's name was not written in the Lamb's Book of Life, he was thrown into the lake of fire. Truth is truth, no matter what *we* think."

If our lifestyle is believing—and passing on—false information, incorrect biblical interpretations and even heresies, we unwittingly are aiding Satan's side of the battle between him and God, not Jesus' side.

Jesus is our absolute source of truth. Not only did He speak *the* truth, Jesus said of Himself, "I *am* the truth" (John 14:6, italics added). Jesus *is* truth personified.

So, we must make sure it is Jesus' voice we are hearing. When Pilate said to Jesus, "So, You are a king?" Jesus replied, "You say correctly that I am a king. For this I have been born, for this I have come into the world, *to bear witness to the truth. Everyone who is of the truth hears My voice*" (John 18:37, italics added). Where? How? In the Bible!

I know this may be an over-simplification, and there are some imponderables in the Bible. But making the Bible—not people—our final authority eliminates most disagreements about what truth really is.

But, most importantly, we must *live* truth. If we have not "put on" truth, no matter what we say or preach, we have left ourselves wide open to the attack of the supernatural evil powers. And then there is no promise from God of our "standing and withstanding" defensively with such a huge gap in our armor.

2. Breastplate of righteousness. The second piece of God's defensive armor we are to put on in order to stand is the *breastplate of righteousness*. The breastplate was metal used to protect the front of a soldier, and even horses and elephants of war. It specifically covered the heart. It was like the bullet-proof vest of today.

And having put on the breastplate of righteousness (Ephesians 6:14).

The putting on of the righteousness of Ephesians 6:14 is not the righteousness given to us at salvation, because those who are to put on the armor already are saved. So it is not its usual meaning of "the righteousness of God through faith in Jesus Christ for all those who believe" of Romans 3:22 whereby people are brought into right relationship with God.

No, the armor's righteousness is something believers *do*. It is "putting on" and "taking up." It is how believers *live* (Titus 2:12). This is the righteousness Christians *pursue*.

But flee from these things, you man of God; and *pursue* righteousness, godliness, faith, love, perseverance, and gentleness (1 Timothy 6:11).

This, again, is not some of God's righteousness automatically falling down from heaven and draping itself around us. It is the believer's personal righteous *lifestyle*.

Having put on the breastplate of righteousness is *obeying* the sum total of God's requirements. Righteousness is the believer's personal *lifestyle* of Romans 6:12 and 13:

Therefore do not let sin reign in your mortal body that you should obey its lusts, and do not go on presenting the members of your body to sin as instruments of unrighteousness; but present yourselves to God as those alive from the dead, and [present] your members as instruments of righteousness to God.

It is frightening to realize that without this righteous lifestyle, we have left ourselves wide open to Satan's attacks, and trying to lead a non-believer into a life of righteousness out of Satan's kingdom is foolish indeed.

3. Feet shod with the preparation of the Gospel of peace. The third item of God's armor is "having shod your feet with the preparation of the Gospel of peace" (6:15).

Since this word "preparation" literally means a pedestal or a base,[1] this is a foothold for *standing,* not a preparation for running. This is still a part of the defensive reason for the armor in Ephesians 6.

It is easy to confuse the two different roles of the feet in the new Testament. While in Romans 10:15 the beautiful feet are of those who *bring* glad tidings of good things to others; here the feet are of the soldier *standing* steadfastly in personal spiritual warfare. This is a *defensive* stance. If a warrior is to "stand," he must have no unprotected and uncertain foothold.

So what, then, is this peace that protects that part of the body in the Christian's spiritual battle? It is the peace the soldier has *with* God through justification at salvation (Romans 5:1), and the peace *of* God which guards our hearts and minds in Christ Jesus (Philippians 4:7).

It also is the peace that comes from the assurance that "He that is within you [Jesus] is greater than he that is in the world [Satan]" (1 John 4:4). It is the incredible peace that comes from knowing our ruler, Jesus, is victorious—and that we can have complete confidence in being able to stand in Him.

People frequently ask me if I'm not afraid to enter the battle with Satan in addressing and writing about his tactics. "No," I tell them. "The greater the stress of the battle, the more an almost tangible peace seems to settle in my innermost being. It almost feels like a huge, immovable chunk of granite anchoring me in the spiritual warfare." Peace!

But we have our part to do. The peace is available to every Christian, but we must avail ourselves of it and put it on. We can't run around barefoot and not expect to get shot in the foot sooner or later.

4. The shield of faith. Next in the armor for our defensive stance is *taking up the shield of faith*.

In addition to all, taking up the shield of faith with which you will be able to extinguish all the flaming missiles of the evil one (Ephesians 6:16).

In Paul's day, the armies would shoot arrows with their tips wrapped in or filled with burning material (like a modern flame-thrower). They would shoot them from slack bows so that the speed would not put out the fire.

The type of shield Paul uses here is not the little light, circular shield that could be moved about easily, but it was a large quadrangular shield, approximately 2½ feet by 4 feet. It was like a door behind which the soldier could take refuge and was the ultimate in Roman warfare protection.

So our shield of faith is designed by God to intercept and extinguish the fiery darts of Satan. His fiery darts are those temptations designed to cause us to sin, thus making us ineffective or completely useless in our spiritual battle against him. *But our faith is the shield standing between us and him that will extinguish them all.*

Faith in what? Our armor? Fellow soldiers? Expertise in using our weapons? Oh, no. Faith in God—resolutely relying on Him for deliverance from temptation.

But the Lord is faithful, and He will strengthen and protect you from the evil one (2 Thessalonians 3:3).

The Ephesians 6 promise when we take up and practice this faith is overwhelming: "you *will* be able." There is no room for questioning. Not "perhaps you will be able" or "you might be able." Unequivocally, unconditionally, you *will be able* to quench all the flaming missiles of the evil one.

And the promise is not just for some, but *all* the fiery darts. When we take up this piece of armor and live in immovable faith, every single one of Satan's fiery darts can be quenched. Extinguished. Not just temporarily or partially smothered, only to flare up at the least little wind fanning it. This is one of the greatest promises in the whole Bible.

However, our part is to get a firm hold on this promise, and stand—in faith—on it. Our faith that will extinguish all these fiery darts must be a *lifestyle* of absolute, unwavering conviction that God not only is able to deliver us,—but *will* deliver us from the evil one.

It is faith in the *victory* that already is ours. That is, the victory in our risen and exalted Jesus over all the powers of that diabolical general of the besieging army, Satan.

5. Helmet of salvation. The last piece of defensive armor we are to take is the *helmet of salvation*.

And take the helmet of salvation (Ephesians 6:17).

"Take" literally means we "receive from the hands of another" the helmet of salvation. It is taking for oneself all that Christ in His saving work offers. Jesus in His death on the cross made available salvation to all, but we must reach out and take it personally to ourselves.

This helmet of salvation gives us Jesus living in us. My heart breaks at how many people are trying to escape Satan's power without having a personal relationship with Jesus. When I teach them I clearly say, "If you do not have Jesus living in you, I have no hope for you. I will not deceive you and tell you there is hope for you against Satan—unless you have Jesus living in you. Only He has power over Satan!"

How foolish to struggle to protect ourselves with a lifestyle of truth, righteousness, peace, and faith without the most important piece—the helmet of salvation. It is only through Jesus we can have all the pieces of armor—since *Jesus* is the truth (John 14:6), righteousness is through faith in

Jesus (Romans 3:22), it is His peace *Jesus* left with us (John 14:27), and we live by *faith in the Son of God* (Galatians 2:20, italics added.)

THE OFFENSIVE WEAPON OF THE ARMOR

All of the pieces of armor so far in this list are *defensive,* and we are expected to protect ourselves by using them before going into offensive warfare against Satan. However, the next item of armor is not defensive but an offensive weapon.

6. Sword of the Spirit.

"And take . . . the sword of the Spirit, which is the Word of God' (Ephesians 6:17).

A sword always was used offensively. It hung from a girdle on the left side of a soldier, ready to be grasped to aggressively attack the enemy. Since it is an *offensive* weapon, we know that our stance is not to be just defensively protecting ourselves but attacking our enemy Satan.

When Satan attacks us, we either yield or fight. And God has provided our sword of the Spirit so we won't have to succomb—but fight. It is to be used offensively by us to silence our enemy Satan. The assailant himself is to be assailed.

I used to wonder how hiding God's Word in my heart could keep me from sinning against God (Psalm 119:11). But the answer is simple. It is not a sin to be tempted, only when we yield does it become sin. And the sword with which we counter-attack Satan's temptations is the Word of God.

But, unless we have hidden that Word in our hearts before the temptation hits, we won't be equipped with that sword with which to thrust at Satan. So we get prepared for the temptation by reading, studying, memorizing, and meditating on the Word of God. Then immediately when Satan sends one of his fiery darts of temptation our way, we counterattack with God's words from the Bible.

But we must practice using this weapon—the Word of God—just as a soldier practices wielding his sword. When the temptation comes, we must learn to say what Jesus said to Satan at His temptation, "It is written . . . ," and then, as Jesus did, quote words from the Scriptures. (See Luke 4:1-13.) The Word of God silenced Satan then, and it will today.

We should use specific quotations for specific temptations as Jesus did. It is wise to memorize Scriptures that have to do with victory over our personal weaknesses, since we know in advance those usually will be the areas the fiery darts will hit.

However, I also frequently am surprised at when and where they hit. Recognizing them often is not easy, as Satan disguises them in things that seem right, taste good, feel good, and often make me temporarily feel good. But as soon as I recognize them as fiery darts from Satan, I take up my biblical sword—and practice James 4:7: "Resist the devil, and he *will* flee from you."

Satan's fiery darts at times are devastating, life-ruining sins. But I find in my life they usually are incapacitating missiles of anxiety, pride, fear, judgmentalism, wrong priorities, indecisiveness, or negativism. When they hit, I find myself getting angry at Satan, and grabbing my sword of the Spirit, the Word of God, to counterattack him. "Satan," I say through clenched teeth, "the Bible says . . . " Then I frequently add, "You have no right to do this to me. Jesus is living in me, and 'Greater is He that is in me than you in the world.' Get out!" And, amazingly, he leaves!

But here too it takes unequivocal faith and trust in the Bible and in its author, God. We cannot ever waver in this counterattack.

Here are some of my most frequently needed Scriptures against Satan: When he wants me to think my world is falling apart, I just say, "Satan, Jesus said, 'My peace I give to you.' Get out!" And the peace of Jesus flows over me. "Be anxious for nothing" calms my racing heart. "Not to think of himself more highly than he ought to think" overcomes the temptation to be proud.

When Satan tries to tell me it's too dangerous or too risky to speak up for Jesus, I quote "Whosoever shall be ashamed of me . . . the Son of Man will also be ashamed of him." And one that seems to stop Satan's fiery darts in mid-air is my favorite: "Satan," I explode at him, "the Bible says 'Be ye holy for I am holy!' "(1 Peter 1:16).

The armor's sword to attack Satan came directly from the Lord Himself. Remember, all Scripture is given by inspiration of God (2 Timothy 3:16), and the Holy Spirit was the conveyor of the Word to the writers of the Bible. They, in turn, wrote it down for us (2 Peter 1:21). And God's Word is just as sharp and powerful today as the day it was penned on parchment.

One of Satan's best tools to defeat us is to keep us out of the Word of God. He knows if we don't have that offensive weapon ready to charge him, we will have to cower defensively trying to protect ourselves while he attacks over and over again. But if we wield the Sword of the Spirit, the Word of God, decisively and effectively against him, we will quench all of his fiery darts.

7. Prayer. The last item of the Ephesians 6 armor is *prayer*.

However, Paul was calling only those clothed with the other pieces of God's armor to pray in the spiritual battle. Why? Because being clothed with His armor is a lifestyle. And it is lifestyle that determines whether or not we get answers to prayer—a lifestyle of doing what is pleasing in God's sight.

> And whatever we ask we receive from Him, *because* we *keep* His commandments and *do* the things that are pleasing in His sight (1 John 3:22, italics added).

(Chapters 7 through 10 of this book will be devoted to this spiritual warfare praying.)

There are two kinds of prayer in the armor of God. The first is prayer for each other personally in Ephesians 6:18:

> With all prayer and petition pray at all times in the Spirit, and with this in view, be on the alert with all perseverance and petition for all the saints.

The other is prayer in proclaiming the Gospel to the lost still in Satan's kingdom in 6:19-20:

> And pray on my behalf, that utterance may be given to me in the opening of my mouth, to make known with boldness the mystery of the Gospel, for which I am an ambassador in chains; that in proclaiming it I may speak boldly, as I ought to speak.

So this prayer is not only defensive armor for the personal safety of other Christians, it is the source of power for the battle for souls against Satan.

So there we have it—all the defensive armor we ever will need to protect us from the schemes of the devil, and the offensive sword and prayer to counterattack him directly. The secret of being "strong in the Lord, and in the strength of His might" has been revealed to us. And we can be equipped to stand and withstand, no matter how fierce the battle with Satan ever becomes.

And then, with all the armor securely in place, the Christian is equipped and ready to enter—safely and victoriously—into the battle of rescuing souls from Satan's evil kingdom.

----

(1) *The Cambridge Bible for Schools and Colleges,* "Epistle to the Ephesians," University Press, Cambridge, London, England, 1895, page 155.

There is something much more dangerous about not being clothed with God's armor than just being vulnerable to Satan's attacks. *It is possible for Christians actually to clothe themselves in the garb of Satan.* Since there are only two spiritual kingdoms, we deliberately must choose which clothing we will put on and which we will take off—God's or Satan's.

As I stood looking at a suit of armor in Edinburgh Castle in Scotland, I puzzled over how any human body could squeeze into that restrictive suit of metal. And I realized how little clothing would fit under it—certainly not a suit of the enemy's armor! It is impossible to put on two sets of clothing or armor at the same time.

Standing there surrounded by rows of ancient armor, my mind went to the spiritual armor of Ephesians 6. I wondered about trying to wear that spiritual armor of God over the things of Satan with which we frequently clothe ourselves. Since it is not possible physically, is it possible spiritually, I wondered? Or are there things God expects us to "put off" in order to "put on" His armor?

Yes, there are. The Bible is just as clear about the pieces of spiritual armor we must "put off" as those we should "put on." They are the *practices* from Satan which God calls *sin*.

And they must be removed before we can put on God's holy armor. Trying to put on an outward covering of God's armor to cover the sin in our lives will not work.

In trying to hinder us in our evangelism efforts, Satan not only aims his attacks at the gaps and missing pieces of our spiritual armor, but he tries to get us to wear his battle array instead of God's.

Entering spiritual warfare for the souls of those still in Satan's kingdom while clothed with Satan's instead of God's armor is foolish indeed, for it deprives us of the protection to stand and withstand Satan. So, it is imperative that we "put off" the sins with which we have clothed ourselves so that we can "put on" God's armor. Only then will we Christians be protected from Satan for the spiritual battle.

PUT OFF

The words translated "laid aside" in Colossians 3:9 literally means "stripped off as clothes or arms."

> Do not lie to one another, since you *laid aside* the old self with its evil practices (italics added).

In Colossians 3:8 the words "Put them all aside" literally mean "to put off from oneself."

Ephesians 4:25 admonishes us to "lay aside" (take off) falsehood—a sin. Again, verse 31 uses the same idea with "put away" which means taking off all bitterness, wrath, anger, clamor, and slander with all malice. All these are sins from Satan with which we clothe ourselves when we practice them.

The same word is used by James in 1:21 where he says, "Therefore, *putting aside* all filthiness and all that remains of wickedness." And Peter uses it in 1 Peter 2:1, "Therefore, *putting aside* all malice and all guile and hypocrisy and envy and all slander" (italics added). Again, take off those sins!

Romans 13:12 says it so clearly: "Let us therefore *lay aside* the *deeds* of darkness and put on the armor of light" (italics added).

THE OLD SELF

What should we strip off? The *old self* with its evil practices. The Bible is very explicit about what sins of the former life a Christian should "take off."

In Colossians 3:1-9 Paul explains that since we have been raised up with Christ, we should consider the members of our earthly body actually dead to immorality, impurity, passion, evil desire, and greed, which amounts to idolatry.

And in them you also *once walked, when you were living in them.* But now *put them all aside:* anger, wrath, malice, slander, and abusive speech from your mouth. Do not lie to one another, since you *laid aside the old self with its evil practices* (3:7-9, italics added).

Also Ephesians 4:22 tells us Christians to "lay aside" (take off like clothes) the *old self* which is being corrupted in accordance with the lusts of deceit. This deceitful lifestyle belongs to your former life—before you accepted Jesus as your Saviour and Lord.

And you *were* dead in your trespasses and sins, in which you *formerly* walked according to the course of this world, according to the prince of the power of the air, of the spirit that is now working in the sons of disobedience. Among them we too all *formerly* lived in the lusts of our flesh, indulging the desires of the flesh and of the mind, and were *by nature* children of wrath, even as the rest (Ephesians 2:1-3, italics added).

But these are the things of the *former manner of life* when they were still walking according to the prince of the power of the air, Satan—which Christians should "put off from oneself."

The Bible says, since you now are a Christian, stop practicing those sins of your former evil life!

A soldier is identified by his uniform. If we have clothed ourselves with Satan's array of a sinful lifestyle instead of

God's holy lifestyle, people will not be able to tell whose side we are on. If our lifestyle is much the same as theirs—defeated, powerless, and evil—we won't have much of a chance to convince them they should change spiritual kingdoms.

COUNTERPARTS OF "ARMOR ON"

Satan has his *opposites* for the pieces of God's armor for us to put on. They are the same as the lifestyle of those still in Satan's kingdom of darkness. These opposites were the way Christians lived *before* they accepted Jesus—not after.

1. Untruth is Satan's opposite of God's truth. Jesus clearly told the Jews who were not of God what the source of untruth was: Satan.

> You are of your father the devil. . . . He does not stand in the truth, because there is no truth in him. Whenever he speaks a lie, he speaks from his own nature; for he is a liar, and the father of lies. But because I speak the truth, you do not believe Me (John 8:44-45).

Peter identified the source of Ananias' lying in Acts 5:3: "Why has Satan filled your heart to lie to the Holy Spirit, and to keep back some of the price of the land?"

So when we indulge in untruth of any kind, we are obeying Satan, not God. And we are clothing ourselves in Satan's lies, not God's truth. We are commanded in God's Word to lay aside (take off like clothing or armor) all untruth.

> Therefore, *laying aside falsehood,* speak *truth,* each one of you, with his neighbor, for we are members of one another (Ephesians 4:25, italics added).
> Do not *lie* to one another, since you *laid aside* the old self with its evil practices (Colossians 3:9, italics added).

Truth is hard to find these days in government, courts of law, school morality, corporation ladder climbing, and even some Christian counseling.

Have you felt it was all right to tell "little white lies," to "tell things the way you want them rather than the way they really are," or to deliberately deceive a family member, co-worker, or Christian brother or sister? If so, there is no way you can be protected with the truth of God's armor—on top of a lifestyle of falsehoods.

In the spiritual battle it is not possible to be "expedient" warriors and "effective" warriors at the same time. In order to have our loins girded about with truth of God's armor, we must take off—as we would undesirable clothing or armor—all deceit, lying, and exaggeration.

2. Satan's unrighteousness is the opposite of the righteousness of God's armor. It is absolutely impossible to be wearing the two at the same time, so Satan's unrighteousness must be taken off by the Christian.

But this is *lifestyle,* not the righteousness of God we became in Jesus when we accepted Jesus as Saviour and Lord (2 Corinthians 5:21). The Book of Ephesians was written to those who already had the righteousness of God *imparted* at salvation. (See Romans 3:22.) So, since the righteousness of the Ephesians 6 armor is the righteousness which *Christians* "take up" and "put on" and is that righteousness which we "pursue" after becoming a Christian, Satan's opposite unrighteousness must be taken off, abandoned.

But flee from these things, you man of God; and *pursue* righteousness (1 Timothy 6:11, italics added).

Romans 6:13 says so clearly that once we become Christians we are to change our *lifestyle* from Satan's to God's.

And do not go on presenting the members of your body to sin as instruments of *unrighteousness;* but present yourselves to God as those alive from the dead, and your members as instruments of *righteousness* to God (italics added).

That word "instrument" means "weapon." In other words we are not to go on presenting our bodies to sin as weapons of unrighteousness but as weapons of righteousness to God!

The lists of sins in the Bible are frightening. Ephesians 5 names the ones that must not be named among Christians: immorality, impurity, greed, filthiness and silly talk, coarse jesting, deceived by empty words. "For because of these things the wrath of God comes upon the sons of disobedience. Therefore do not be *partakers* with them" (Ephesians 5:3-7, italics added).

Let us *behave* properly as in the day, not in carousing and drunkenness, not in sexual promiscuity and sensuality, not in strife and jealousy. But *put on* the Lord Jesus Christ, and make no provision for the flesh in regard to its lusts (Romans 13:13-14, italics added).

Paul gives a list of things we should *put away:* falsehood, giving place to the devil, stealing, unwholesome words, grieving the Holy Spirit, bitterness, wrath, anger, clamor, slander, and all malice. (See Ephesians 4:25-31.)

These are awesome lists of sins. *And practicing one of them, or any other sins listed in the Bible, is substituting Satan's garb for the breastplate of righteousness of God's armor—leaving us unprotected for our spiritual battle.*

For many years I have been aware that I have a personal responsibility when giving an invitation to those in Satan's kingdom to accept Jesus. I have learned from experience that I cannot have a known sin in my life—and then see God powerfully move in an audience. Speaking at a denominational statewide convention last month, I planned to give these church members the privilege of making sure Jesus was their personal Saviour and Lord. But early that morning, it took an hour and a half alone with God in prayer before I felt I was ready, or eligible, to do it. Begging God to search my heart and find any wickedness in me, I asked Him to cleanse everything that would hinder the Holy Spirit from working that day. It is futile for me to try to battle Satan for souls while he has a toehold in me.

I warned the campus pastor of a Christian college that it was extremely dangerous to enter into spiritual warfare with

Satan without being protected by God's armor. It was after midnight when a student who had been accompanying our singing with his guitar asked for help because he was obsessed with hard Satanic rock music. He was devastated because, though he frequently burned his diabolical tapes and sheet music, he could not keep himself from buying more. Before praying with him, I asked that pastor if there was any known sin in his life. Shocked, he quickly confessed every one he could think of. And we proceeded to pray with this student—because he then could be protected with God's breastplate of righteousness after taking off Satan's counterpart.

We cannot have the protection of God's armor and wear Satan's unrighteousness at the same time. So, before attempting to enter into spiritual warfare for souls still captive in Satan's kingdom, make sure you have taken off Satan's unrighteous lifestyle and put on the righteous lifestyle of God's armor.

3. The opposite of the helmet of salvation of God's armor. This opposite is much more frightening than just not being protected as a Christian. *It is not being a Christian at all.* Unless we have put on the helmet of salvation, we still are in Satan's evil kingdom of darkness.

Putting on the helmet of salvation transfers us out of Satan's kingdom of darkness and into the kingdom of God's dear Son, Jesus.

For He delivered us from the domain of darkness, and transferred us to the kingdom of His beloved Son, in whom we have redemption, the forgiveness of sins (Colossians 1:13-14).

Satan's spiritually fatal lie is convincing people they have put on the helmet of salvation while, in fact, they have not. There is no way they ever can have the protection of God's armor while they still belong to Satan's kingdom.

While in a country in Central America this spring, I spoke to the pastors and church leaders of most of the denominations in that country at their annual convention. I boldly asked any who were not sure to pray out loud asking Jesus to come in as their personal Saviour and Lord. And to my astonishment, they prayed all over the room. Of the fifteen in the first row facing me, six of them prayed that prayer. They had been deceived by Satan into thinking they already had the helmet of salvation on when they didn't. Now as I write, that country is plunged into civil war and some of their religious leaders are being martyred. How grateful I am that I bothered to ask such a seemingly foolish question to that leadership group.

Jesus said these shocking words to the hypocritic and lawless religious leaders of His day, "You serpents, you brood of vipers, how shall *you* escape the sentence of hell?" (Matthew 23:33, italics added) Though these scribes and Pharisees appeared righteous to people, they obviously had not put on the helmet of salvation Jesus required.

Striving to "put on" God's lifestyle of truth, righteousness, peace, and faith is absolutely futile until the helmet of salvation has been put in place. Leaving the head exposed not only makes that vital part of the body vulnerable, but it actually deprives the warrior of any life in Jesus.

It is not what we say, but what we live that proves whether or not we have on the helmet of salvation. If we *consistently practice* the deeds of the devil, we need to examine our helmet of salvation. (See 1 John 3:7-10.)

4. The opposite of the peace of God's armor. Satan has his counterfeits for the *peace of God's armor,* but we can only win in the spiritual battle if we are standing firm in God's peace.

Since the peace of God's armor is the peace that is produced *in* the believer, that can only come after there is peace *with* God--which comes at salvation. This is the moment someone from Satan's kingdom puts on the helmet of salvation.

Therefore, having been justified by faith, we have peace *with* God through our Lord Jesus Christ (Romans 5:1, italics added).

Today there is a frantic search for peace in the whole world. Because people everywhere are feeling a deep spiritual void, Satan is right there to fill the vacuum with his pseudo peace. And people by the billions on planet earth are turning in desperation to these false sources of peace.

- *Eastern religions* have been eagerly espoused in recent years in the western world as they promise peace through meditation, mantras, and oneness with the universe.
- The *New Age Movement* is rapidly filling this tremendous spiritual void with their pseudo peace of contacting thousands-of-years-old entities through channeling, with out-of-body experiences, and with contact with the extra-terrestial world.
- The *occult* world had its first great explosion in America in the early 1970s, and has grown at a phenomenal rate since then as people are searching for spiritual reality, which they do find in these occult practices. But it is Satan's temporary, pseudo peace—leading to eternal destruction—not God's real peace.
- Peace through *drugs*—illegal and prescription—has become a way of life in these days. Whenever people are too up, or too down, when they can't cope, or when reality is too painful—there is an escape into the false peace of drugs.
- The *dying* are searching for peace. Our nursing homes and hospitals are full of apprehensive and sometimes terrified people wondering what is on the other side of their imminent death. But giving nice little programs, bringing cupcakes or flowers, or desensitizing them with drugs will never solve their problem. They still are on their way out to a Christless eternity. There is no peace unless they have a chance to make their peace *with* God.
- Civil wars and uprisings to change the ruling regime are seen as the *political answer* to peace. Speaking to the Christian students at Wits University in South Africa recently, I talked about the futility of the struggle there. "No matter whom you elect in next week's election," I told them, "no

matter how many times you revise your national constitution—it will never bring real peace. The only hope for South Africa—and the whole world—is Jesus. He alone can bring peace."

This is peace in spite of spiritual battles with Satan and sometimes because of them. Frequently after an unusually hard or long battle with Satan is over, I find myself just relaxing in God's presence—with His sweet peace flowing over me like sweet, warm oil.

In order to put on God's real peace, we must take off all the false sources of peace. As long as we are clothing ourselves with any or many of these imitations, there is no way we can put the peace of God's armor on top of them. No, they must be completely removed before the peace of God can be ours and we stand firm with our feet shod with this peace.

5. The opposite of the shield of faith. Satan has been very clever and successful in getting people to substitute faith in *things* for faith in *God*.

There is no real shield against today's flame throwers of Satan except faith in God. Only He is able to turn back and quench these fiery darts when we use our shield of faith in Him.

But Satan is trying to convince us just the opposite, consistently succeeding in getting Christians to trust in temporal, worldly, and even pagan things.

He has succeeded in getting students to put their faith in their *education*—only to find upon graduation there is a glut of qualified workers in their specialty and no job openings.

Many a marriage partner has been convinced by Satan to put all their faith in a *spouse* instead of in God, only to discover there is someone else who is number one in their mate's affection—or life.

Our daughter, Jan, speaking at Bethel College chapel about her profession as a critical care doctor, told those students of the suicide attempts she gets called to handle in the middle of the night. "And," she told those students, "it usually is because they have broken up with a *boyfriend* or *girl-*

friend or lost their *job*, and they had nothing to live for." Misplaced security and faith.

Satan has been tremendously successful in telling people their *profession*, not God, is where they should put their faith. But then comes the crash with a financial reversal in their company or somebody discovering something new that suddenly makes what they know and do obsolete.

Satan also gets many Christians to put their faith in their *families*—only to have a child break their hearts as they denounce the family value system. Or embarrass them by their rebellious lifestyle. Or commit suicide. Misplaced faith in loved ones, rather than in God, is often devastating.

Our Nancy just told me of a friend whose husband is divorcing her. She is horrified because she'll lose her security—her *house*. Nancy gently told her that, although losing her home is heartbreaking, her security still could be in her God. How sad she had let Satan fool her into putting her faith in material things for her security—instead of in God.

One of Satan's clever ploys is to get Christians to put their faith in their *pastor* rather than God. And then, if he falls into sin as so many are doing these days, their faith in the whole system of Christianity and in God Himself falls with the pastor.

Of course, Satan really has won when people put their faith in his *doctrinal heresies* instead of in Jesus, the truth. How frequently he convinces people that: "It's not *what* you believe, but your *sincerity* in believing it that counts," or "All religions should be respected equally," or "You'll have another chance when you are reincarnated in your next life." Faith in such falsehoods has sent millions of people straight to hell.

Many of these things which we substitute for faith in God are intrinsically evil. But the confusing part is that some of these may be good in themselves. They only get people in trouble when trusting in *them* is substituted for faith in *God*.

But it is only faith in the all-wise, all-powerful God of the universe that can provide a shield against the fiery darts of the evil one, Satan. It is the kind of unmovable faith in God that makes me clench my fists and grit my teeth when I feel the scorching of Satan's fiery missiles as he tries to deter me in my spiritual battle.

So we must make sure we take up the *real* shield of faith—in God—so we can stand defensively against Satan's attacks. All others melt, collapse, or are pierced by Satan's fiery darts.

HOW DO WE TAKE OFF SATAN'S BATTLE ARRAY?

Are you saying, "I'm really serious about getting rid of the things of Satan in my life, but *how* do I go about it?"

There are definite fool-proof steps:

1. The first thing is to be able to *identify* the weapons and the tactics of the enemy. When my husband was a bomber pilot in World War II, he and his crew had to undergo intensive training to identify enemy aircraft. They had to know the planes from all angles—just by getting a split-second glimpse of the silhouettes. And they diligently studied the way the different planes behaved, for sometimes it was the only way they could catch that it was an enemy aircraft.

So, where can the Christian study the weapons and tactics of the enemy Satan? In the Bible, of course. In this chapter there are only some of the many, many weapons and tactics of Satan which are clearly identified and explained in the Bible. There are many more for you to discover for yourself. So, keep searching, studying, and learning from God's Word. Then, when reactions, thoughts, intentions, or a coarse of action comes to your mind, you will automatically identify the source—Satan or God.

2. The next step in taking off Satan's battle array is *staying in tune with the Commander in Chief* as He sends warning signals and commands. Not paying attention to a military commander—or ignoring his communications—can be deadly to a soldier. Same with the Christian. We must listen to the Lord in our prayer times and stay sensitive to Him at all times—ready, even eager, to catch the faintest warning or the shrillest command.

3. Then, *believe the Commander in Chief,* not the enemy, when He tells us something is sin.

One of Satan's most diabolical lies is, "That *used to be sin;*

but now we know, in this age of enlightenment, that it isn't sin anymore." While in high school our daughter asked me one day, "Mother, is it still sin today what was sin when you were a young girl?" Together we turned to Ephesians where she was reading devotionally to find the answer to her question. It only took a few minutes of reading for her to discover that we are to be holy and blameless before God, and He hasn't changed His rules or requirements since before the foundation of the world.

Another lie of Satan is, "Oh, that really isn't *sin*." And gullible soldiers of God's army fall for these lies, until they go down in defeat when the enemy's fiery dart lands.

Attending the events connected with the most recent Presidential Prayer Breakfast in Washington, D.C. was an exciting time for me. First, Billy Graham stopped by our table at one of the dinners and said, "Oh, hello Evelyn!" I beamed and had a warm fuzzy feeling in the pit of my stomach. Next, Chuck Colson came by escorting a newly appointed member of the President's cabinet. As she bubbled her "How good it is to see you again," I warmed from head to toe. Then at the Presidential Prayer Breakfast itself, the wife of another member of the President's cabinet closed in prayer. Having read an interview where she told how her life had been changed by my *Lord, Change Me* book, I eagerly struggled through the crowd to shake her hand. But as she gave me a big hug—and the secret service personnel quickly moved in—I really was thrilled.

I left immediately to fly to Florida for an evening banquet and the next day's seminar. And there in the airport was Joni—who threw that arm around me she has learned to move with muscles that still work in her shoulder. "Oh, Evelyn," she cried, "it's *so* wonderful to see you!" By this time I decided these were some of the best days in my life. All those wonderful people!

As I settled back in my plane seat, basking in the Washington events, immediately God struck me with, *"Evelyn, that's sin. The sin of pride!"*

I was devastated. On the whole trip to Florida I struggled

with my sinful attitude, admitting and confessing it to God. But somehow I couldn't settle it in my heart. I was unnerved knowing that a spiritual battle for souls awaited me in that banquet hall. So though people were being seated and there wasn't time for the usual prayer with the committee prior to my speaking, I sent word to the chairman to get some committee members to my room immediately. "Please pray for me," I told them. "I'm struggling with an attitude that God has told me is sin." They supported me in prayer while I prayed and God forgave. And I went cleansed to that banquet—where people all over the room prayed to accept Jesus that night.

When I told my husband my reaction to those great people and God's reprimand, he said, "Well, that doesn't sound like *sin* to me."

"Tell the Lord that!" I retorted. *"He* calls it sin!"

The only way to avoid being cut down by enemy fire in our spiritual warfare is to believe our Commander, the Lord, in His infallible Word, the Bible.

It is a very wounded soldier who thinks his commander is kidding, or isn't capable of really identifying the enemy. But the soldier finds out very quickly that the commander was right when the ammunition starts finding its target: him or her!

4. *Admit we have put on Satan's garb.* There is no Christian eligible to wear God's armor because of never having put on any of Satan's sin. The Epistle of 1 John was written by the Apostle John to *Christians,* and He said to *them* in 1:8: "If *we* say that *we* have no sin, we are deceiving ourselves, and the truth is not in us" (italics added).

We must admit that what we are doing is sin in God's eyes—not just a short-coming or personality weakness. Sin! (See James 4:17.)

5. Last, the crucial step in getting rid of Satan's garb is *doing something about that sin.* But what should we do?

Since all Satan's garb with which we clothe ourselves is called *sin* by God, it only can be removed by being *forgiven by God.*

How? The unconditional rule for getting rid of that sin is the Christian *confessing* it to God.

If we *confess* our sins, He is faithful and righteous to forgive us our sins, and cleanse us from all unrighteousness (1 John 1:9, italics added).

Confessing means identifying the sin specifically. And then repenting—which means being devastated by that sin, as Peter was when he went out and *wept bitterly* after denying his Lord Jesus. The basic meaning of the word repent is "to turn away from," and this is extremely important in keeping ourselves free of Satan's sinful garb.

The rest is up to God. He forgives.

READY FOR COMBAT

And when God forgives, the guilt of that sin is removed, and Satan's armor is removed from the Christian so that God's can be put on.

Without the protection of God's armor it is sheer folly to enter into evangelism's battle for souls. And it also is foolish to think we can wear the two sets of armor at the same time—God's and Satan's.

As long as we Christians are clothed with Satan's sinful lifestyle, we will be open, defenseless, and powerless against Satan's fiery attacks.

It is only when we Christians have taken off all Satan's inhibiting sins with which we have clothed ourselves, that we can put on God's armor. And only then are we protected and equipped to go forth into the spiritual battle of rescuing captives from Satan's evil kingdom.

SEVEN
EVANGELISM PRAYING—
ON THE OFFENSIVE
Ephesians 6:19-20

While Satan is working feverishly to take every-body to hell with him, must Christians sit helplessly by and let Satan *keep* all those people who were born into his kingdom? Is there nothing we can do except protect ourselves defensively from him while he tightens his grip on those already lost? Or is there an OFFENSIVE battle Christians can—and should—take up?

I learned quite by accident in the early '70s, how to fight *offensively* with Satan for souls. I was doing a Bible study series in the Minnetonka Baptist Church and had asked if anyone wanted to accept Jesus. Several prayed with the usual joy of becoming a new creation in Jesus. All except one. Hilarie (name changed) tried to pray, but couldn't. So I invited her to stay with me after the others had left.

Alone in a little room we knelt to pray. I expected the same response as usual; but, to my amazement, she absolutely could not pray asking Jesus into her heart. She tried and tried, but would look at me with anguish in her eyes and cry, "I can't!" Then she would try again. And I would pray. And she would pray. She went limp as she dropped her head on the chair where she was kneeling. She could not accept Jesus.

Suddenly a light dawned. I felt an unbelievable anger toward Satan surge over me. How did he have the audacity to keep my class member out of Jesus' kingdom? I spewed out my condemnation of him—directly to him. (It was not prayer. I do not pray to Satan. I was just telling him off in no uncertain terms.) "Satan," I snapped, "you have no right to do this to Hilarie. I claim the *blood* and the *name of Jesus of Nazareth* against you. You *must* leave. You have absolutely no right to hinder her any longer. Jesus died and shed His blood for her. He already has bought her back from you. You *must* leave."

Immediately something seemed to pop. The bondage was gone. She was free. With ease she prayed asking Jesus to be her Lord and Saviour. She was radiant as she lifted her tear-stained face to mine, beaming a great big smile. Free in Jesus!

I realize now that God was teaching me several major lessons *experientially* (which I already knew theologically). He let me experience first hand the tenacious struggle of Satan trying to hold on to someone in his kingdom. I felt his tentacles almost wrapping around her, trying to keep her from leaving him for Jesus. I watched as she tried and tried, but was somehow hindered by an unseen force—Satan.

God also powerfully taught me that I could not do anything about breaking that power in my own strength or human efforts.

But then God taught me what *could* break Satan's hold—*the name and blood of Jesus*. It did work to take the *initiative* and step out to battle Satan. It did work to go on the *offensive* against Satan in soul-winning! I was joining the victorious Jesus in His *offensive* war with Satan for lost souls!

THE BLOOD OF JESUS

The Roman soldiers at the cross drove nails in Jesus' hands and feet and, because Jesus was already dead, they did not break His legs—as customery—but instead plunged a spear into the side of the Son of God (John 19:34). But they must have been totally unaware what they had done. When the blood flowed from Jesus' hands and feet and when His blood and water came gushing out from His side, those soldiers not only had fulfilled the prophecy of Zechariah 12:10—*but they had unleashed the irresistible force of the universe: Jesus' blood!*

It was that blood which would provide the power for the spiritual battle for souls. It was that blood which would justify sinners in Satan's kingdom and save them from the wrath of God (Romans 5:9). It was that blood which provided forgiveness of sins at redemption (Ephesians 1:7). That blood was the power for believers to overcome the accuser of the brethren—Satan (Revelation 12:11). That blood was the blood that released us from our sins (Revelation 1:5).

Peter explained that our offensive battle for souls is in the power of the blood of Jesus shed on the cross.

> "You were not redeemed with perishable things like silver and gold from your futile way of life inherited from your forefathers, but with precious blood, as of a lamb unblemished and spotless, the blood of Christ" (1 Peter 1:18-19).

SPIRITUAL OFFENSIVE WEAPONS

Since this battle is strictly spiritual, weapons of human intellect and power never can bring victory. When Paul described our armor for this supernatural battle in Ephesians 6, he quickly pointed out that our struggle is not against flesh and blood, but against *spiritual beings*. So we must use spiritual weapons and spiritual power in this offensive battle.

> For our struggle is not against flesh and blood, but against the rulers, against the powers, against the world forces of this darkness, against the spiritual forces of wickedness in the heavenly places (Ephesians 6:12).

Paul also clearly explained this in 2 Corinthians 10:3-4: "For though we walk in the flesh, we do not war according to the flesh, For the *weapons* of our warfare are not of the flesh, but *divinely powerful* for the destruction of fortresses" (italics added).

But what are our *offensive* spiritual weapons? What is the *offensive* spiritual power available to Christians? P-R-A-Y-E-R!

Two Kinds of Warfare Praying

Ephesians 6:10-20 teaches there are two kinds of spiritual warfare praying—*defensive* (verse 18) and *offensive* (verses 19 and 20). Just as there are defensive and offensive tactics in sports, so there are in the spiritual battle.

In *defensive* tactics, the players try to defend and protect themselves and their goal line from the onslaught of the opposing team rushing offensively against them. Likewise, in defensive praying the Christians pray for each other for protection in our mutual spiritual battle against Satan.

But *offensive* tactics are just the opposite of defensive. There the players rush against the opposing team to score points. It is the same in offensive spiritual warfare praying. There the Christians invade Satan's territory "to score" by releasing those captive in his kingdom.

If there are only *defensive* plays in sports, the score would remain at a 0 to 0 tie, and nobody would win. To win in sports there must be offensive plays. And so it is in the spiritual battle for souls. There must be *offensive* plays—and prayers—if we are to rescue the lost from Satan's kingdom.

In that Ephesians 6 description of the spiritual battle, why did Paul tell Christians to put on God's armor? *Only* so they could stand firm against the devil's schemes? *Only* so they could be safe from Satan's fiery darts? *Only* so they could stand—still? No. Paul concludes the armor portion with Christians actively *doing* something—*counter attacking Satan* with the Sword of the Spirit, the Word of God—and *praying*.

Jesus' Offensive War

Today Satan has two sets of battle tactics—one for unbelievers (to keep them captive in his kingdom) and a different one for Christians (to keep them ineffective in the spiritual battle of rescuing souls). Most of the Christian books and seminars these days address only Satan's tactics *against Christians* and our *defensive stance* in Jesus against him. While this is true and very necessary in order for us to do what Jesus has called us to do, we must remember that the war Jesus is waging against Satan is an *offensive* war.

Jesus *offensively* is battling for those still captive in the kingdom of darkness where they were born. On the cross He paid the price for their redemption, but they still personally must switch kingdoms by believing in Him. So Jesus is actively engaged in battle—going after those He paid the price on the cross to redeem with His blood.

And Jesus expects us to help Him. Of course, no human can "save a soul." (Only God can do that.) Yet Jesus has called Christians to be on the *offensive* against Satan for the souls of the lost. But how? What is our part?

Evangelism—empowered by prayer!

EVANGELISM'S OFFENSIVE PRAYING

Paul concluded the Ephesians 6 armor section with a plea for Christians to pray a specific *offensive* prayer for himself.

And pray on my behalf, that utterance may be given to me in the opening of my mouth, to make known with boldness the mystery of the Gospel, for I am an ambassador in chains; that in proclaiming it I may speak boldly, as I ought to speak (Ephesians 6:19-20).

He wanted prayer for more than just his being able to stand firm; he asked for prayer for his *offensive* battle attack against Satan. He was aggressively, offensively *"making known with boldness the mystery of the Gospel."* Hearing and believing the Gospel of Jesus, of course, is the only way people can get out of Satan's captivity.

Paul was asking for prayer to accomplish the task for which he was called on the Damascus road. Jesus had told Paul the purpose of his call was "to open their eyes so that they may turn from darkness to light and from the dominion of Satan to God" (Acts 26:18). Paul's was a call to *offensive* action—to transfer souls from Satan's to Jesus' kingdom.

And this too is the *offensive* task Jesus has given to all of us. In His Great Commission Jesus commanded us to go make disciples (of Himself) of all nations (Matthew 28:19). And we, as much as Paul, need offensive prayers for this task.

How Do We Pray Offensive Prayers for Souls?

First, we need to understand the enemy's tactics and then practice the kind of prayer that defeats him. One of Satan's main devices in keeping people captive in his kingdom is *deceit*.

He tries to fool people into thinking they are real Christians—especially Bible-studying members of fine churches—when they are not. Jesus said, "Not everyone who says to Me, 'Lord, Lord,' will enter the kingdom of heaven." Even to those who prophesied in His name, cast out demons, and in His name performed many miracles Jesus will say, "I never knew you. Depart from Me" (Matthew 7:21-23).

Many years ago I learned a *simple procedure* that produces amazing results when giving an invitation to accept Jesus—or make sure He is Saviour and Lord. Even though most of my seminar participants around the world belong to a church, I've learned not to assume they are all real Christians. So just before I give an invitation to accept Christ, I confront Satan directly about his deceiving them.

While the participants are praying in their small groups, I take the opportunity to pan the whole audience, looking briefly at each person in the room. Then I silently address him with, "*Satan, you have deceived these people long enough. Jesus died for every person in this room, and you have no right to deceive them, Satan, I am claiming the* blood *and the* name *of* Jesus *against you. I command you to leave, because you cannot stand against Jesus' name and His blood!*" (See Revelation 12:9-11.)

And the great dragon was thrown down, the serpent of old who is called the devil and Satan, who deceives the whole world . . . *and they overcame him because of the blood of the Lamb* and because of the word of their testimony (italics added).

Then I turn to the Lord in prayer, asking Him please to save them—every one. Continuing to look over the audience, there is a deep aching in my heart for those dear ones sitting out there, lost. My praying for them feels like when I travailed in birth for my babies—struggling, longing for their birth. Re-birth in Jesus! "Father," I cry, "woo them, draw them, open their hearts to Jesus! Save them, please!"

Was this what Paul felt when he too cried, "Brethren, my heart's desire and my prayer to God for them is for their salvation" (Romans 10:1).

At our Friday night prayer meeting before my Saturday all-day seminars, I teach the interdenominational seminar committee to address Satan. Together we claim Jesus' name and His blood against Satan's deceit of those who will be attending the next day. Then we go into intercessory prayer for all those who will be there the next day, praying that not a single one will leave without being absolutely sure that Jesus is Saviour and Lord.

And it works! Since 1980 when I started doing this, I've been averaging at least 25 percent of every audience of church members praying to make sure Jesus is Lord and Saviour.

At last Saturday's prayer seminar sponsored by churches from several counties, approximately half of the audience prayed, making sure Jesus was their personal Saviour and Lord. Two weeks ago, people had driven from nine states to attend the seminar in Indiana. And somewhere between one-half and three-fourths prayed immediately when I gave them a chance. Satan and his deceit cannot stand against the name and blood of Jesus!

Recently I was conducting a training session for the prayer leaders of an upcoming evangelistic crusade to be conducted by one of Billy Graham's assistants. I thought it was foolish to ask people like those eager leaders to pray to accept Jesus as their personal Saviour if they weren't sure they had, so I skipped that part of the teaching. However, God gave me no rest until I backed up and asked them to pray it—just in case. But I was almost in a state of shock when all over the room those leaders prayed, making sure Jesus was their personal Saviour. And they were there to learn how to teach others how to pray for souls in their evangelistic crusade. How Satan had deceived them!

RESPONSES

There are many different kinds of responses in my seminars' small prayer groups when people realize they most likely don't have a personal relationship with Jesus. The kind of praying they do varies from seminar to seminar and geographic area to area.

Occasionally there is an awkward hesitation while everybody waits for someone else to start, and then the number swells as more and more join in around the room. Sometimes they seem almost embarrassed to admit in front of other Christians that they aren't sure of their personal relationship with Jesus. Then the praying is so soft I almost have to watch to see the lips moving as I strain to hear their voices. Frequently it is excited, eager praying—gaining momentum as it swells in a great crescendo. And there are times it is like the seminar in Phoenix where there was an immediate explosion of those prayers throughout the audience. And one lady threw her arms in the air and cried out, "Oh, Jesus, You *know* I want to accept You as my Saviour!"

At my "What Happens When God Answers" seminar in New York City in 1988, people of every imaginable race and color had packed the auditorium and filled the TV overflow room at a downtown Manhattan church. When I gave the invitation to accept Jesus, people cried out to the Lord all over that building. I almost thought I was going to have to "put a lid" on the response—as they praised God with shouts, weeping, and stomping of feet.

But the best part of this victory in their small prayer groups is the members spontaneously throwing their arms around the new members of the family as the tears of joy flow. Transferred out of Satan's kingdom!

DIANE'S STORY

My close friend, Diane, grew up in the church my husband pastored, and she has been one of my most faithful pray-ers for years.

Here's her account of one of her experiences in this battle for souls against Satan:

I had only been going into the county jail for about six months, but the woman who had trained me was a fifteen-year veteran of jail ministries. Two things she had drilled into my head: (1) Satan was alive and thriving in the jail community and therefore authority over him *must preceed* even going there. (2) Every woman had a need to know Jesus as her Saviour, and the *only* obstacle to that relationship was Satan.

With these two understandings I pulled up a chair in a guarded, closed-off room. Across the table was a 5' 10" stocky Indian woman. She was a seasoned convict and jail had been her home off and on for ten years. I only knew of her—as her reputation had circulated in even the most conservative circles.

As I looked into her cold, dark eyes, I must admit to feeling a bit uneasy. "Yeah, what do you want?" she sneered as she lit her cigarette.

"Tonja, I just wanted to talk with you and introduce you to my friend, Jesus," I answered.

"Yeah?" she half asked. "Well, I've had a lot of time to think about Him. I heard that He loves me. I've tried to pray, but somehow I can't. I don't know what's stopping me from asking Jesus into my heart, but something inside of me is saying, "no!""

I had watched Tonja's body language as she had spoken. Physically she had become extremely tense. Her hands were clenched, and when she had finished talking she emphatically pounded the table. I knew what the obstacle was; I had seen this before. It was almost tangible. It was Satan!

"Tonja, I'd like to pray; and when I'm through, I believe you'll be ready to accept Jesus, OK?"

"Sure," she answered.

"Father, in the name of Jesus I believe for You to convict Tonja by your Holy Spirit. Jesus, I believe for You to be her Saviour today. Satan, in the name of Jesus I command you to take your hands off Tonja. You've had your way with her long enough. She is about to become a child of the King. In the name of Jesus, release your hold on her! Thank You, Father. In Jesus name, amen."

I looked up at Tonja. She was shaking from head to toe. "Tonja, you are free now to accept Jesus into your heart."

"I think you're right," she replied. "I don't feel that tug of war anymore inside of me."

We bowed our heads and Tonja prayed the sinner's prayer. When we had finished, I couldn't help but notice the visible tranquility on her face. It was as if I was looking at a totally different person. Tear flowed down from her beautiful black eyes . . . eyes that had just seen Jesus!

She gently brushed the tears from her cheeks and surprised me by her question. "Now are the angels up in heaven having a party?"

Yes, there is *offensive* praying for souls that really does produce results. First we must recognize that all people who haven't accepted Jesus as Saviour and Lord are still in Satan's kingdom, and he is tenaciously hanging on to every one of them. Then confront Satan with the power of the *blood* and the *name* of Jesus—and do battle in offensive, attacking prayer.

Satan does not easily give up his prey!

Offensive spiritual warfare praying—against Satan—right *while* we are introducing people to Jesus really does work.

There is much praying we need to do *before* we actually try to introduce people to Jesus. Sometimes long, extended prayer is needed to prepare the heart and mind of a person captive in Satan's kingdom. This too is *offensive* prayer, but it is not the same as the claiming the blood and name of Jesus *as* we lead someone to Jesus. This is asking God to become involved *before we do*. It is the praying that makes lost people *receptive* to the Gospel and *able* to accept Jesus.

Many Christians conscientiously are witnessing, going as missionaries, teaching, preaching, and faithfully giving invitations to unbelievers to accept Jesus—but are puzzled at their lack of results. However, the Bible tells us one of the reasons *why*. It is the well-planned and carefully-executed plan of a super-natural being—Satan. It is Satan's evil strategy to keep Christians from invading his kingdom and convincing his subjects to transfer out of his kingdom into Jesus' kingdom.

Understanding Satan's reason and tactics makes us able to plan and execute our own offensive tactics against his wicked schemes. We then can pray and involve the God of the universe on our side as we strive to win the lost to Jesus.

SATAN AND THE GOSPEL SEED

In the parable of the sower Jesus gave us one of the reasons the gospel seed doesn't bring forth fruit in unbelievers. He said some seed fell beside the road, and it was trampled under foot, and the birds of the air ate it up (Luke 8:5). Then, explaining the parable to His disciples, Jesus said:

> The seed is the Word of God. And those beside the road are those who have heard; then *the devil* comes and takes away the Word from their heart, so that they may not believe and be saved (Luke 8:11-12, italics added).

Satan knows the power of the Word of God. He knows that people are "born again, not of seed which is perishable but imperishable, that is through the living and abiding Word of God" (1 Peter 1:23). So one of his main tactics in keeping people in his kingdom is to snatch that Word before it can take root in their hearts.

In other words, when we share, preach, or teach the Word of God, Satan is right there snatching up that seed. And our efforts have been in vain. Nothing happens because the seed of the Gospel did not take root.

But Satan only can do this if the soil is hardened—like that beside the road in Jesus' parable. So, how do we solve that problem of these hardened hearts? We pray!

We must *precede* the sowing of the seed with intense prayer. We need to pray specifically that God will go ahead of the seed and prepare the hearts of those who will hear. Pray for them individually, by name if possible—for their hearts to be softened. Then when the Word of God comes, that seed can take root instead of being gobbled up by Satan. And those we are trying to reach for Jesus will be saved.

For many years our organization has been reaching millions who still are in Satan's kingdom with broadcasts to all of China, a large part of India, and now to all Spanish speaking people in the Western Hemisphere over Trans World Radio. But only recently have I been teaching my pray-ers about Satan's plan to be there when the Gospel comes over the airwaves to their radios. So now I am asking those supporting the broadcasts in prayer and financially to pray for God to *prepare the hearts of those He knows will be tuning in*—so that Satan can't snatch the Word of God of our Gospel broadcasts. I tell them all of our money and effort in broadcasting will be wasted if we don't stop Satan from gobbling up the seed as fast as we transmit it to their radio receivers.

After I shared this thought at a conference recently, a pastor said to me, "Now I understand why I can preach my heart out and not see any souls won to Jesus. I need a new kind of praying in my church. Praying *before* I preach!"

MINDS BLINDED BY SATAN
Another tactic of Satan about which we should pray is his *blinding the minds of those who are perishing* (2 Cor. 4:3-4).

And even if our Gospel is veiled, it is veiled to those who are perishing, in whose case the god of this world has blinded the minds of the unbelieving, that they might not see the light of the Gospel of the glory of Christ.

"The perishing" are those who are still in Satan's captivity because they have not been transferred out of Satan's kingdom into Jesus' kingdom. They are those who will spend eternity in hell with Satan instead of in heaven with Jesus.

And the "god of this world" is Satan. He is the one who has blinded the minds of unbelievers. Again, our sharing the Gospel will be in vain if their minds are blinded to it. So it is absolutely necessary to involve God *before* we try to win them to Jesus. We need to pray for God to remove the blinders Satan is keeping so securely in place on the lost.

God *does* open their minds. When Paul went to the riverside in Philippi looking for a place of prayer on the Sabbath, he found a group of women. As he taught them, the Lord opened Lydia's heart to respond to the things spoken by Paul (Acts 16:14). She became the first convert Paul won in Europe. But it was *the Lord* who opened Lydia's heart.

How can we get God to open the hearts of those we are

trying to win to Jesus? By praying. Though God is sovereign and moves as He pleases, prayer definitely activates God's working in unbelievers.

Second Corinthians 4:4 was the Scripture a close pastor friend used to break the hold Satan had on a medical doctor as he was struggling in the pastor's office. The doctor's search had taken him through a deep study of secular philosophies, and he had been trained in the doctrine of the church into which he was born. Finding inconsistencies and discrepancies in what they taught, he sought out my pastor friend.

"I can't believe. I want to, but I can't!" the doctor cried.

The pastor asked him if they could pause to pray. "In the middle of the prayer," the pastor told me, "I just said: 'In the Name of the Lord Jesus Christ, I bind Satan from blinding you to the light of the Gospel of the glory of Christ.' "

As soon as the pastor finished praying, the doctor calmly said, "I want to receive Christ." And he did!

This is *offensive* spiritual warfare praying—asking God to remove Satan's veil that is blinding the minds of those we are trying to win to Jesus.

SEEING THE LIGHT—JESUS

The removing of the blinding of the mind results in "seeing the light." Second Corinthians 4:4 also says Satan blinds "that they (unbelievers) might not *see* the *light* of the Gospel of the glory of Christ." Satan is desperately trying to keep his captives from seeing the light of Jesus, so *one of his main tactics is to blind them to the light of Jesus.*

Again it is the battle between the *kingdom of darkness* and the *kingdom of light.* But Jesus came as the light of the world. The Prophet Isaiah prophesied, "The people who sit in darkness will see a great light" (Isaiah 9:2). Then the prophecy was fulfilled in Jesus. "The people who *were* sitting in darkness saw a great light" (Matthew 4:16, italics added). Jesus!

I am the light of the world; he who follows Me shall not walk in the darkness, but shall have the light of life (John 8:12).

People are transferred out of the kingdom of darkness into the kingdom of light when they accept Jesus. The Christians in Ephesus were told, "You were *formerly* darkness, but *now* you are light in the Lord" (Ephesians 5:8, italics added).

In Paul's call on the Damascus road, Jesus said the purpose was "to open their eyes so that they may turn *from darkness to light* and from the dominion of Satan to God" (Acts 26:18, italics added).

However, those living in the kingdom of darkness do not see the Light because they are blinded by Satan. So what can we do about their not seeing the Light, Jesus? We can pray!

Praying for blinded eyes is *offensively* demanding that Satan remove the blinders. We must claim the blood and name of Jesus against Satan—and then ask God to bring the light of Jesus into them.

WHAT CAN I DO?

Are you asking, "This seems so complicated. What can *I* do?" The answer is that *you don't have to be a full-time expert in spiritual warfare to get involved in offensive praying for souls.* The prayers of ordinary Christians can be, and usually are, the power behind people being led to Christ. Every time you pray for those still in Satan's kingdom to come to Jesus, you are entering into spiritual warfare with God against Satan.

METHODS OF PRE-EVANGELISM PRAYER

Here are some simple methods *any* Christian can use effectively in offensive praying for souls:

● As an **individual** it is possible to set aside time to pray for those you, or others, are trying to reach for Jesus—and then to pray specifically, faithfully *by name* for them to be released from Satan's captivity.

I can still see my almost ninety-year-old (now deceased) board member Edith sitting in board meetings with a little pile of pictures in her lap. She couldn't stand it until she had shown us that month's pictures. Of what? Children, grand-children, birthday parties, vacations? Oh, no. Missionary friends from her "special mission field" regularly sent her the names and pictures of those they were trying to win to Jesus. Edith would then pray, by name, for them *until they accepted Jesus*. In her sleepless, painfilled nights, Edith often prayed all night. The pictures were that month's harvest of her converts! Her pain-ridden wrestling for those souls was the power that produced their release from Satan's evil kingdom.

● It was a **pastor** of a large, rapidly growing church in California who told me that every Saturday night he walks through the huge church sanctuary and personally touches every pew, praying for God to start working against Satan in the hearts of the people who will be sitting there the next morning. Pre-evangelism praying—before he preaches and gives the invitation to accept Jesus in the Sunday morning service.

● My **mother** spent her lifetime praying for lost family members and people in her town. In her quiet, humble way she carried on a relentless spiritual battle with Satan for souls. When she died, it was said of her that she won more souls to Jesus than anybody else in the whole town—in addition to all the members of her extended family. Transferred out of Satan's kingdom because a stubborn little lady wouldn't give up. Is there somebody *you* love who has not accepted Jesus?

And it was Ruth, my **evangelism Bible study hostess** way back in the 1960s, who prayed for her lost neighbors *before* inviting them to our evangelism Bible study in her home. She would walk around the blocks, praying and asking God at each house if that occupant was ready to come to our Bible study and accept Jesus yet. When she felt He was saying "Yes, they're ready. I've prepared them," she would knock on their door and invite them. Then, while they attended the Bible study designed specifically to introduce them to Jesus, Ruth spent hours a week praying *by name* for their salvation—doing spiritual battle with Satan for their release from his captivity. And all but two who came to that evangelism Bible study those three years accepted Jesus (or made sure they had a personal relationship with Him). God prepared their hearts ahead of time because Ruth prayed!

● There is great power in **husband and wife teams** praying for the lost to be transferred out of Satan's evil kingdom. While my husband pastored our church in Rockford, Illinois, one of our couples became managers of a large apartment building across town. Little did we know that they had decided to win people to Jesus that way. They fervently *prayed by name* for each tenant in their building to find Jesus. Then they started home Bible studies and showed Jesus' love by doing nice things for those tenants. One Sunday two whole pews in our church were filled with people from that apartment building. When my husband gave an invitation to accept Jesus—or join the church if already a Christian—the whole two rows of people stood up in unison and came forward to declare their new-found faith in Jesus! New members of the kingdom of God's dear Son—because somebody cared enough to fight a spiritual battle in prayer for them.

● A very powerful tool for evangelism is **church prayer groups.** But amazingly, we basically pray for other Christians in our church and small group prayer meetings. Praying for each other certainly is not wrong, but it is puzzling to me why we spend over 90 percent of our praying for sick Christians who, when they die—and they will—will go to heaven with Jesus. And we spend virtually no time praying for those lost people who, when they die, will spend eternity in hell. How simple, and rewarding, it is to add to our list of prayer requests those who are lost, pray by name for them week after week, and then have the joy of seeing them turn to Jesus. Transferred out of Satan's kingdom because we prayed!

That is the secret behind the largest church in the world. Dr. Paul Yonggi Cho's church in Seoul, South Korea, has well over a million members. And new members basically are from their *small house church groups* where they pick out neighbors and friends who still are lost in Satan's grasp. Then they persistently pray for them by name to find Jesus—until they do and join the church. Also about 10,000 members are at prayer for souls *while their pastor preaches!* This is an extremely effective method of spiritual warfare for the lost souls of a city!

● One of *the most effective,* yet simplest, methods of pre-evangelism prayer I have seen is **triplet praying.** It works amazingly well in churches, prisons, place of employment, neighborhoods, and on campuses. All it takes is three Christians willing to discipline themselves to pray every week for the salvation of people still captive in Satan's kingdom.

Triplets produced the greatest results Billy Graham had had up to his 1984 Mission England crusades where 90,000 Christians in England formed into groups of three for *pre-crusade praying.* Each of the three Christians chose three non-Christians, and then *got together* once a week for the year preceding the evangelistic Crusades and *prayed by name* for their nine to find Jesus. The January, 1989 *Decision* magazine, encouraging triplet sign-ups for Billy's 1989 Mission England II, reported that many of the prayer triplets saw all nine for whom they were praying accept Jesus *before Billy even got there!* With over 7,000 churches each having many, many triplets for Billy's Mission England '89, the results were earth-shattering. What a powerful way to battle Satan for souls in a whole nation!

● Sig, Lorna, and I as **prayer partners** had a triplet from 1964 to 1968 (although we didn't call it that), and saw many for whom we wrestled in prayer week after week come to Jesus. One summer we decided to pray for each boy individually *by name* in the 4th grade boys' class of our Vacation Bible School to accept Jesus while I was their teacher. We hung on tenaciously in prayer through those two weeks, and every boy accepted Jesus by the end of that school. Spiritual warfare praying for their souls!

● The large percentage of people praying to accept Jesus during my seminars is due, not only to my commanding Satan to leave while I give the invitation, but equally because of the **pre-seminar praying of committees.**

We request our interdenominational seminar committees get together *to pray* six months before I come and pray together at least weekly just before the seminar. Many of the committees pray through their registration list, interceding specifically *by name* for each registrant. Many pray over each pew in the church where attendees will be sitting. All of the committees pray for everyone who will attend—that *not one* will leave the seminar without being absolutely sure he or she has accepted Jesus personally. So there has been spiritual warfare over those souls months before I get there—to reap the harvest.

Then on the Friday night before the seminar when I lead the committee in prayer, we do something special. Together we ask God to cleanse the auditorium or sanctuary of all previous Satanic activity. We claim the blood and name of Jesus against any untruth that has been taught there and all sinful thoughts and acts that may have been committed in that building. We ask God to send the cleansing blood of Jesus through that place, ridding it of all of Satan's influence. Next we ask God to fill that room with His holy presence—and power for those who will be attending the next day to be released from Satan's deceit and binding tactics—so they will be free from Satan's hold and free to accept Jesus.

(For a fuller coverage of intercessory prayer methods, see *What Happens When Women Pray* and *What Happens When God Answers* by the author.)

SUPERNATURAL BATTLE

Though you already are praying for the salvation of lost people, there may be a missing dimension in your pre-evangelism praying. Since a supernatural being is involved when we pray for them to be transferred out of Satan's kingdom into Jesus', it is necessary to make sure we are using the *supernatural power* available to us.

"For though we walk in the flesh, we do not war according to the flesh, for the weapons of our warfare are not of the flesh, but divinely powerful for the destruction of fortresses. We are destroying speculations and every lofty thing raised up against the knowledge of God, and we are taking every thought captive to the obedience of Christ" (2 Cor. 10:3-5).

We must be sure to claim the name and blood of Jesus against Satan while we are doing battle in this spiritual warfare for souls. It is Jesus who defeated Satan once for all on the cross by shedding His blood, and Satan *must* release his captives when the force of Jesus' blood attacks him offensively.

> And the great dragon was thrown down, the serpent of old who is called the devil and Satan was thrown down to the earth and his angels were thrown down with him. And I heard a loud voice in heaven saying, "Now the salvation, and the power, and the kingdom of our God and the authority of His Christ have come, for the accuser of our brethren has been thrown down, who accuses them day and night. *And they overcame him because of the blood of the Lamb* (Revelation 12:9-11, italics added).

There is a phenomenal supernatural power struggle in this battle for souls as Satan tenaciously hangs on to his subjects, and God just as tenaciously battles to set them free.

The committee in a western U.S. city had prayed four years for the lost in their community before our prayer seminar. And when I gave the invitation to accept Jesus, approximately two-thirds prayed out loud. Several people told me that, when all those people prayed simultaneously to get out of Satan's kingdom, they felt something like a bolt of lightning flash across the room. Much pre-evangelism prayer— much evangelism power!

The local chairman and the international chairman of the large Bible study movement sponsoring me in Australia reported the same thing. Both said that when 50 percent of their audience of 1,000 in Adelaide prayed simultaneously to accept Jesus, they felt like a charge of electricity ran down their backs. Supernatural power!

Since our pre-evangelism praying for souls activates a battle between God and Satan, we must be certain we draw on the supernatural powers that are ours. We must be very sure we pray in the name of Jesus and claim the blood of Jesus— *the totally irresistable force against Satan on earth.* It works.

Jesus came to set the captives free (Luke 4:18), and He does!

NINE
DEFENSIVE PRAYING
AGAINST SATAN
Ephesians 6:18

It is impossible for Christians to keep up their offensive warfare prayers for souls without *defensive* prayers for each other. While our offensive prayers are against Satan as we strive to get captives released from his evil kingdom, *defensive* prayers are for the protection of Christians *from* Satan's attacks. They are for God to deliver *us* from all the tactics of the devil against us.

We need these two kinds of prayer because Satan's battle plan against Christians is just the opposite of his battle plan for non-believers. With *non-Christians,* Satan is on the defense, trying to keep them in his evil kingdom where they already are. But Satan is attacking Christians to make them ineffective in their battle to get those lost souls out of his kingdom.

My husband was a bomber pilot in World War II, piloting his B17 plane *offensively* to drop bombs on enemy targets. But he and other bomber pilots depended heavily on the fighter planes surrounding them—*defensively* protecting them from the enemy's anti-aircraft missiles and guns. So it is in the spiritual battle for souls. While we are on the offensive, we need defensive protection.

The armor of Ephesians 6 which Christians put on for our spiritual battle includes *defensive* prayer for each other (verse 18) as well as offensive prayer for the lost (verses 19-20).

> With all prayer and petition pray at all times in the Spirit,
> and with this in view, be on the alert with all perseverance
> and petition for all the saints (Ephesians 6:18).

Defensive praying is for saints; in other words those who
were justified by being cleansed from all their past sin when
they accepted Jesus as Saviour and Lord—and were transferred out of Satan's kingdom. (See Colossians 3:13-14.) But
these saints obviously have not been removed from the attacks of Satan.

DEFENSIVE PRAYING

I learned *defensive spiritual warfare praying* out of sheer necessity. It was in 1971 when America's first "occult explosion"
was making headlines in our newspapers. The book *The Exor-
cist* was number one on the New York Times bestseller list.
Christians in general were oblivious to the dire consequences
to Satan's power, were choosing to hide behind some theological hangup, or were concentrating only on a "God is
love" mindset.

But God very clearly called me through 1 Timothy 4:6 to
make "these things" (the doctrine *of* demons) known to the
brethren. Then, to my surprise, God started opening doors
with unsolicited invitations to come to Sunday Schools,
youth groups, public and Christian grade schools, high
schools, and even some colleges. Administrators and teachers
wanted their students warned about the dangers of the occult
practices they were doing at Halloween and slumber parties
and in the school bathrooms. So, hesitatingly, I started accepting these invitations.

First, I would show these young people from the Bible
that the supernatural things they were practicing such as oui-
ja boards, "Mary Worth mirror images," levitation, seances,
etc., were strictly through supernatural power from Satan's
kingdom. Then I would ask for a show of hands of those
who right then or, in the recent past, had been involved in
these satanic activities. To my horror, the average was 98
percent—even in church youth groups!

Almost all of them thought it was just fun and games, not having the vaguest idea they actually were plugging into the supernatural power of Satan. So I showed them from Deuteronomy 18:9-13 that any who practiced such things were an "abomination to God." Most of our sessions ended with their asking God for forgiveness, some crying, and many praying to make sure Jesus was their personal Saviour and Lord. Frequently they also disposed of their occult paraphenalia and artifacts.

However, I was in for a shock. Every time I would speak on that diabolical subject, I would be filled with unexplainable feelings of anger and negativism. Finally my family said to me, "Mother, you're not the same person when you speak on that subject." One daughter who was away at college would even call and say, "Mother, I know what you spoke on tonight!"

There were few practical "how to" books written for Christians about the occult back then, and there was very little preaching or teaching about it in the Christian church. So, in desperation, I had to "start from scratch." Realizing the source of my problem was Satan, and knowing only God could help me, I gathered together eight women I knew to be deep women of God. I explained what was going on and asked for their help.

We organized what we still call our "occult prayer chain" with both monthly prayer meetings and a telephone prayer chain. They went to prayer every time I went to speak, claiming the *blood* and *Name of Jesus* over me. And amazingly, the very first time they went to prayer all those awful feelings disappeared. And to this day when I have taught about Satan's kingdom—they never have come back. Defensive praying for me!

DEFENSIVE PRAYING PROVIDES THE POWER
There is no way Christians can stand or advance in the battle with Satan, even when wearing the armor of God, without God providing the power. Our being able to resist the schemes of the devil requires more than human strength and

sheer determination. That is why *defensive* prayer for each other is included in the Ephesians 6 armor.

God never intended Christians to stand alone in their spiritual battle. He provided other Christians to undergird us with prayer in our battle with Satan—as he tries to make us ineffective through temptations and harassment as we battle for souls and witness for Jesus.

Amazingly, prayer is the *part of the armor of Ephesians 6 we usually omit!* And we stand, all dressed up in our armor, yet powerless because we have not utilized the only power source strong enough to withstand our enemy. It would seem foolhardy not to intensify our defensive praying for one another while we are multiplying our offensive soul-winning efforts and prayers. But that is what we so often do.

In my prayer seminars I frequently have the people *practice* this type of prayer in their small groups. Each one selects a pastor, priest, Sunday School teacher, or church leader. First they thank Jesus for providing the power of His blood through His death on the cross. Addressing (not praying to) Satan, they tell him they are claiming the blood and name of Jesus against him—and command him to leave that person. Then they pray a scriptural promise *for* their leader. This is a first for many of them, but their apprehension turns to victory as they pray. Then we stand to sing, "He is Lord, He is Lord. He is risen from the dead, and He is Lord!"

But what *do we pray for each other in this spiritual warfare?*

SATAN'S TACTICS AND GOD'S ANSWERS
Satan uses clever, diabolical tactics to hinder our soul-winning efforts. But there are *scriptural answers to his tactics* which we can pray for others (and ourselves) against Satan's attacks. We can wield the armor's sword of the Spirit—the Word of God—on behalf of other Christians.

However, we first need to *determine and understand the tactics Satan is using against Christians.* Then we must *learn which scriptural answers to pray.* Here are some of Satan's tactics and God's answers.

1. Snare of the Devil. In the past few years, Christian

leaders, evangelists, and pastors in America have been drop-
ping like flies to sexual sins. What, or who, is causing them
to lose their reputations, thus making them ineffective for
Jesus? The Bible tells us it is the *snare of the Devil*.

And he (overseer of the church) must have a good reputation with those outside the church, so that he may not fall
into reproach and the *snare of the devil* (1 Timothy 3:7,
italics added).

A close friend of mine who is an administrator in the
Southern Baptist Convention told me he decided to check
out the rumors about Satan worshipers praying to Satan
against pastors and their wives. So he went to the Atlanta
airport where he found Satan worshipers with their satanic
bibles confronting passengers. He asked them if it was true
that they fasted and prayed to Satan every Friday for Satan to
bring another woman into a certain pastor's life or another
man into his wife's life. They willing answered, "Yes." Then
they named for him the five Atlanta area pastors they had
targeted—whom they felt were the greatest threat to their
master, Satan.

What should we pray? Before praying, we should address
Satan, demanding that he stop attacking Christian leaders.
"Satan, Jesus defeated you on the cross. And they belong to
Jesus. He is living in them. You have no right to harass them.
We are claiming the blood of Jesus against you—in Jesus
name. Get out!"

We then pray for God to cancel the effectiveness of these
satanic prayers. If we would persist in prayer as faithfully *for*
our leaders as the Satan worshipers pray *against* them, we
could turn the tide and stop this onslaught against our
leadership.

A good Scripture to pray is what Jesus taught us to pray in
His model Lord's Prayer: "Our Father who art in
heaven . . . deliver us [ourselves and them] from the evil one"
(Matthew 6:9, 13).

2. Conceit and Falling into Condemnation. The Bible

also gives a warning about immature leaders and the devil: "Lest he become conceited and *fall into the condemnation incurred by the devil*" (1 Timothy 3:6, italics added).

This is not a new problem. The same thing happened to King Uzziah. He became king at sixteen, and as long as he sought the Lord and did right, God prospered him *until* he was strong. Then his heart was so proud that he acted corruptly. When over eighty priests tried to stop him, Uzziah became enraged and continued desecrating the temple, until the Lord smote him with leprosy on his forehead. How often we have seen that happen recently to both our young and our mature Christian television personalities, authors of good Christian books, and successful pastors and priests! Satan sometimes gets Christians in success more than in failure. Success leads to conceit, conceit to arrogance, arrogance to sin, and sin to condemnation and downfall.

Could this be because we have not prayed enough for them? Knowing the source of this conceit, have we consistently prayed for our leaders that they would be able to avoid the condemnation incurred by the devil?

What should we pray? Before praying, we should address Satan and claim the blood of Jesus against him in that person's life, demanding that "in the name of Jesus" he leave that leader. (See Revelation 12:11.)

Then we should pray asking God to keep them alert to the pitfalls according to 1 Corinthians 10:12: "Therefore let him who thinks he stands take heed lest he fall."

3. Fear. Another tactic of Satan against Christians is *fear*. Since God has not given us this spirit of fear, we know it is from the only other supernatural force, Satan.

But God has not given us a spirit of fear, but of love and power and a sound mind (2 Timothy 1:7, KJV).

Since my original occult prayer chain started and now with much organized prayer support for my ministry and me, I truly can say I have no fear in this battle with Satan.

Last summer I was conducting a prayer seminar at a convention in Colorado meeting in the downstairs auditorium of a large hotel complex with no windows or outside doors. So we were oblivious to a severe mountain thunderstorm passing through just as I finished teaching about our power in prayer over Satan. While they were all practicing praying against Satan in their little groups, the electricity suddenly went off, flickered, and then plunged us into pitch blackness. Several screamed in fright as fear seemed to sweep over that auditorium. Satan had used the unknown, though easily explained weather situation, to terrify them while they fought him in prayer.

Afterward, many told me the greatest lesson they learned all day was my complete calm, as I confidently led on in prayer while they were so afraid. But I felt no fear. Why? Because my prayer chains back home were praying. Our committee praying the night before had included asking God to deliver us from the evil one—claiming the blood and name of Jesus over the meeting. And their committee had prayed for months before my speaking there. *The spiritual battle was already fought.*

What should we pray? Pray that all Christians who feel any degree of fear of Satan would get a firm hold on and unequivocally believe "Greater is He [Jesus] who is in you, than he [Satan] who is in the world" (1 John 4:4). This is the Scripture I use more than any other against Satan. Over and over I claim it; I jab at Satan with it. I've even yelled it at him!

A note from one of my most powerful board member pray-ers, a lifetime missionary in Africa, said:

Dear Evelyn:
I thank God for the privilege of "Holding up your hands" in the warfare you now are engaged in. Satan *cannot disturb you* as you write *if we are faithful in intercession.* Praise God! Satan is trembling as you write. He knows we have the victory through our Lord Jesus Christ!
In His love, Edy

4. Accusing the Brethren. Satan also is the *accuser of the brethren.*

> Now the salvation, and the power, and the kingdom of our God and the authority of His Christ have come, for the *accuser of our brethren* has been thrown down, who accuses them before our God day and night (Revelation 12:10, italics added).

The word "devil" in Greek is "diabolos" and means "slanderer or accuser." It is used thirty-five times in the New Testament (including the being who accosted Jesus on the Mount of Temptation).

Slandering and accusing before God—and before people—is one of Satan's most powerful *tactics* in destroying our effectiveness for Jesus. This has been one of Satan's main tactics against me in my ministry.

Once my publisher phoned telling me I should call Australia immediately because there was a problem with my upcoming seminars they were sponsoring there. I was in for a shock. Someone had told them that my husband and I were into bizarre practices—and if this were true, my appearance there would be canceled.

After they believed that these accusations were absolutely unfounded, I wondered about their source. Though I was quite sure of the human who had felt it her duty to inform them of the rumors she had heard, the real source of this slander was obviously Satan himself—using a Christian to pass on his accusations.

After arriving in Australia, I realized why Satan was nervous enough to go to all that bother. He was desperately trying to hang on to those people in Australia who were still in his kingdom and who would be attending my seminars. However, never less than 25 percent of those audiences prayed to accept Jesus. They were transferred out of Satan's kingdom into Jesus' kingdom anyway!

Why didn't Satan's slanderous tactic work? Because my 24-Hour Prayer Clock was organized specifically for that trip.

Through it a thousand people across the United States were linked in prayer around the clock during the whole Australian tour.

How do we pray when Satan slanders with untruth? The answer follows the Revelation 12:10 Scripture that identifies the devil as our accuser: "And they overcame him because of the blood of the Lamb and because of the word of their testimony" (Revelation 12:11). Claim the blood of Jesus against not only the slander but the effects it will have against ministry for Jesus.

5. Tempting Christians to Sin. One of Satan's main tactics in the spiritual battle is *tempting Christians to sin,* thus making them ineffective warriors against him.

I also sent to find out about your faith, for fear that the *tempter* [Satan] might have *tempted you,* and our labor should be in vain (1 Thessalonians 3:5, italics added).

Satan even tempted Jesus, trying to thwart His ministry on earth. But we have a wonderful promise in Hebrews 2:18. Because of Jesus' own temptations, we have hope in our temptations. "For since He Himself [Jesus] was tempted in that which He has suffered, He is able to come to the aid of those who are tempted."

What should we pray for Christians being tempted? First, tell Satan to get out. Then thank Jesus that He understands, and ask Him to come to their aid. Next, a good Scripture to pray for them in *their part* in Satan's temptations is what Jesus told His sleeping disciples during His agony in Gethsemene: "Keep watching and praying that you may not enter into temptation; the spirit is willing, but the flesh is weak" (Matthew 26:41).

6. Holding Captives. Satan *holds captives, to do his will.* We must correct those who are in opposition, so that God can grant them repentance leading to the knowledge of the truth, and "they may come to their senses and escape from the snare of the devil, *having been held captive by him, to do his will*" (2 Timothy 2:26, italics added).

What to pray for them? Opening His earthly ministry, Jesus went to His childhood synagogue, and read from Isaiah 61: "He has sent Me to proclaim release to the captives . . . ." Then He made this startling proclamation, "Today this Scripture has been fulfilled in your hearing" (Luke 4:18-21).

First, we pray thanking Jesus that in Him captives are set free. Then we address Satan that, since Jesus on the cross accomplished setting those captives free, Satan has no right to bind them in his yoke of slavery again. (Galatians 5:1)

7. **Thwarting Christians in Ministry** is a powerful tactic of Satan. Even Paul had this problem: "For we wanted to come to you—I, Paul, more than once—and yet Satan thwarted us"(1 Thessalonians 2:18).

The word "thwart" means "putting something on the road or breaking up the road in front of travelers." These are the obstacles Satan put in our way to keep us from doing God's will, especially when we are rescuing people from his clutches.

What to pray when this happens today? We have a promise in James 4:7 that we can claim whenever Satan tries to hinder and thwart our activities: "Resist the devil, and he will flee from you" (James 4:7b).

The eleventh chapter of my book, *Lord, Change Me* deals with the subject of one of the sources of wisdom producing our personalities—the demonic source. The woman editing it was the assistant editor of the "Decision Magazine" at the time, and was unusually qualified. However, after trying and trying, she could not edit that chapter. Finally she called me and admitted her frustration. "I'll get help," I assured her. I called my board telephone prayer chain—which was already praying through every word and problem of getting that book published.

They went to prayer at once, claiming the blood and name of Jesus over her and asking God to deliver her from the evil one. (See John 17:15.) Immediately she sat down and breezed through editing the chapter. No longer hindered by Satan!

Satan uses many ways to thwart our activities for Jesus. He

used a physical thorn in the flesh on Paul. (See 2 Corinthians 12:7-9.) He tried to thwart our videotaping my "Lord, Change Me" seminar in South Africa for their distribution. Before the seminar I spent from 6 to 8 A.M. in the bathroom with a violent attack of diarrhea from parasites. But the local committee wrestled in prayer for me while my 24-hour Prayer Clock continued unbroken in the States. When I stood up to teach, God answered all those prayers. I had more power than I knew what to do with—not mine, but Christ's upon me—as I stood before the cameras from 9 A.M. until 4 P.M.! Satan's thwarting was thwarted by prayer!

8. Prowling like a Roaring Lion. Another tactic of Satan is to *prowl around like a roaring lion* trying to find some Christian to devour. He is not prowling for those already in his kingdom. He is *our* adversary, not theirs.

> Be of sober spirit, be on the alert. Your adversary, the devil, prowls about like a roaring lion, seeking someone to devour. But resist him, firm in your faith (1 Peter 5:8-9).

What do we pray? The answer is in the same verses as Satan's prowling tactic. When we have stayed alert and caught Satan, we pray resisting him in the name and blood of Jesus—holding on unwaveringly in faith that Jesus is stronger that Satan.

Someone said to me recently that in her area they now know that, though Satan is still prowling like a roaring lion, he now is toothless—a harmless old lion. Sorry, but Satan still is the Prince of Darkness, the god of this world, the evil one! And he must be resisted actively and with prayer.

9. Leading Minds Astray. This is a crafty tactic of Satan. Our minds are the battlefield of Satan. Most of his fiery darts land there, and by influencing our minds he controls us.

> For I am jealous for you with a godly jealousy; for I betrothed you to one husband, that to Christ I might present you as a pure virgin. But I am afraid, lest as the serpent deceived Eve by his craftiness, your minds should

be led astray from the simplicity and purity of devotion to Christ (2 Corinthians 11:2-3).

What to pray? We must pray to bring every thought captive to Christ.

For though we walk in the flesh, we do not war according to the flesh, for the weapons of our warfare are not of the flesh, but divinely powerful for the destruction of fortresses. We are destroying speculations and every lofty thing raised up against the knowledge of God, and we are taking every thought captive to the obedience of Christ (2 Corinthians 10:3-5).

While teaching Satan's tactics to my adult Sunday School class, we did a little experiment. Using the second hand on a watch, we closed our eyes to see how long we could keep our minds under control and exclusively on Christ. We discovered that it wasn't very many seconds for any of us, as Satan baited us with suggestions of things we *wanted* to think about. We were not inclined to resist the secret longings of our souls—even when we knew they were from Satan. We must reject all thoughts from Satan. An undisciplined mind is wide open to Satan's attack. This includes minds which are out of control because of drugs, alcohol, and hypnosis.

10. Angel of Light Disguise. A very clever tactic of Satan is disguising himself as an *angel of light* in the form of false prophets.

For such men are false apostles, deceitful workers, disguising themselves as apostles of Christ. And no wonder, for even Satan himself disguises himself as an angel of light (2 Corinthians 11:13-14).

Second Timothy 4:3 tells us that the time will come—and obviously it is here now—when people will want their ears tickled. They actually will accumulate for themselves teachers who teach what they want, turning away from the truth. This is Satan's way of getting people to turn from Christ.

However, Jesus is the only true light in the world. "There was the true light which, coming into the world, enlightens every man" (John 1:9). Satan is a counterfeit. He makes things look good and right to us when in fact they are evil.

What to pray? First we need to ask God to give us a spirit of *discernment* so we won't be misled. Jesus said in Matthew 24:4, "See to it that no one mislead you." And then we need to wield the Word of God—the only real truth—in prayer against these false teachers of Satan. We must claim the blood and name of Jesus, and we must *praise*.

When we struggled many hours in prayer against that false teacher in London claiming to be Jesus, Satan's power broke completely when we added twenty minutes of *praise* singing to our prayers. This should be our tactic against the New Age Movement also.

11. Deceit is another of Satan's tactics. He keeps us inactive in soul-winning and ineffective in our witness for Jesus through constant bombardment with his lies. Jesus said, "For he [the devil] is a liar and the father of lies" (John 8:44).

Not only does he lie to those in his kingdom to keep them there, but he deceives Christians into believing his lies and lying themselves. It was Satan who filled Ananias' heart to lie to the Holy Spirit (Acts 5:3).

Satan is the source of all lies. He started with the first lie in Genesis 3:4 telling Eve "you shall not die." But she did die and the whole human race with her.

So, what do we pray? After rebuking Satan, we can pray Colossians 1:9 for them: "We have not ceased to pray for you that you may be filled with the knowledge of His will in all spiritual wisdom and understanding."

12. Satanic Oppression. Another tactic of Satan is *oppressing people*. He knows in that condition we are useless in the spiritual battle for lost souls. Peter gave us these encouraging words about being oppressed by the devil: "You know of Jesus of Nazareth, . . . how He went about doing good, and healing all who were *oppressed* of the devil" (Acts 10:38, italics added).

Last Sunday I heard a local church's service on TV. The pastor's wife told how she had been what doctors called a manic depressive. When no form of deliverance worked more than a day or two, she took her Bible—the Sword of the Spirit. For nine months she read continuously, even hours at night when she couldn't sleep. When throwing up with her bleeding ulcers, she would prop the Bible up on the toilet and read it. Little by little she came out of it. Now, beaming victoriously, she said she is absolutely fine.

What to pray? The answer is right in the Acts 10:38 verse: Jesus. We use that Scripture *against* Satan and *for* the oppressed person. Then we pray that the oppressed person will use *their* Sword of the Spirit against Satan too.

GOD'S PROTECTION FROM SATAN
Against Dangers from Satan. There must be *dangers from Satan* since we are promised to be *protected by God* from the evil one.

> Finally brethren pray for us . . . But the Lord is faithful, and He will strengthen and *protect you* from the evil one (2 Thessalonians 3:1, 3, italics added).

What to pray? Thank God He promised to protect us from the evil one. Then we pray specifically for God to do it.

I desperately needed the protection of God through all the prayers for me by my 24-Hour Prayer Clock and telephone prayer chains while ministering in a Central America country deep in the throes of civil war.

As we arrived in the capital city at 7 A.M., the guerillas had knocked out all the electricity. The streets were full of tanks and soldiers. On the way into the capital from the airport, our host said, "This is a very dangerous time in our country. We are on the road where those three Catholic nuns were ambushed and killed." I glanced at the side of the road as he said, "Do you see those bushes over there? That's where the assassins were hiding."

"Oh, by the way," he added, "be very careful what you say

at that national pastor's conference today. We have it on good authority that the guerillas will be infiltrating your meeting." And they did.

Then on the way back to the airport that night, when we got to that clump of bushes again, the taxi right in front of us was ambushed. They were pulling the people out just as we passed. A cold chill swept over me as I searched the bushes to see if there were more assassins waiting for us. I started to cry out to God, "Oh, Father, protect *us!*"

But God stopped my praying, saying so clearly to me, "You don't have to pray that prayer. You already *are* protected by all that praying."

As I wrote to thank all the pray-ers for their very needed prayers, I told them, "All through my Central America tour, I felt like I was wrapped in a cocoon of prayer. I felt insulated, surrounded, and lifted above the danger swirling around me."

Protection of the Angels. Another important prayer for *protection from Satan* is for God to send His ANGELS.

For He will give His angels charge concerning you, to guard you in all your ways. They will bear you up in their hands, lest you strike your foot against a stone (Psalm 91:11-12).

Satan knows this promise, quoting it when he was tempting Christ on the Mount of Temptation. After he had Jesus stand on the pinnacle of the temple, Satan said to Him, "If You are the Son of God throw Yourself down; for it is written . . . ." Then Satan quoted Psalm 91:11-12.

What to pray? In the spiritual battle between Satan and God, Satan has his supernatural hierarchy of demons at his command, while God has His myriads of angels. These are ministering agents sent by God to help His children.

Are they [angels] not all ministering spirits, sent out to render service for the sake of those who will inherit salvation? (Hebrews 1:14)

When we sense supernatural danger we should pray for the protection of God's angels for one another.

There is a large church on the west coast that is close to a powerful New Age community. While conducting a prayer seminar there, the committee—knowing firsthand the local battle—had set up a special prayer room. They took turns staying on their knees in there, praying throughout the day. After I finished teaching and they practiced "spiritual warfare praying," the pray-er came dashing out from the prayer room. Her eyes were wide with wonder and awe. "Evelyn, I saw angels in an arch around you while you were teaching about Satan!"

Peter didn't know if he was seeing a vision or an angel coming to deliver him from prison. But the angel was real, sent by God to rescue him while prayer was being made for him fervently by the church to God. (See Acts 12:5-17.)

Satan uses any tactic that will make us ineffective for Jesus. A missionary in the Philippines asked me to tell their supporters back home to pray for their children. "Satan gets at *us* through *our children*," she said.

I pray almost every day for my children, my husband, and my four precious granddaughters: "Oh, God, send Your angels to protect them from every onslaught of Satan as promised in Psalm 34:7: 'The angel of the Lord encamps around those who fear Him, and *rescues* them.'"

Hedge of Protection. The Bible also speaks of a *hedge of protection*, and it can be prayed for when there is a need for protection from Satan. A "hedge" in the Bible was a barrier set up to protect a vineyard, orchard, or person from marauders. (See Psalm 80:12-13, Isaiah 5:5, and Hosea 2:6-7.)

While Satan was conversing with God about Job, he accused God of having put a *hedge* about Job. Satan said that was the reason Job trusted God.

Hast Thou not made a hedge about him and his house and all that he has, on every side? (Job 1:10)

In our spiritual battle with Satan, we can pray for God to

provide a hedge, to protect believers from Satan's onslaught and temptations. How often in the midst of particularly difficult or dangerous times I have pictured in my mind God putting a hedge around my board members, friends, or family—as I begged God to protect them from Satan.

VICTORY OVER SATAN'S DEMONS

We are seeing more and more evidence of Satan using his *demons* against Christians. Satan, not being able to be everywhere at once like God, has to have help. So we have him *and* his demons described in Ephesians 6:12.

But Jesus gave us our orders—and privilege—in Mark's recounting of the "great commission."

And these signs will accompany those who have believed: in My name they will cast out demons (Mark 16:17).

I asked a woman in my autograph line at a recent retreat if she could stay until I finished, as I sensed she needed more than a minute's help. I asked a women in prison ministry to join us with her friend Betty. Mona [names changed] had a tremendous struggle trying to verbalize her problem. But we finally understood she had an "escort service" and, when there was not a girl available, she would go herself. Her husband knew and agreed because he liked the money. She was frantic that if she stopped there would not be enough money for the children. She had tried to stop by taking her number out of the last phone book, only to have it reappear mysteriously in the next issue.

I kept asking her, "Can you identify any spirit in you that is not from God?" But, though she tried and tried, she always answered she could not.

When she started to whimper, I put my arm around her shoulder and addressed Satan. I told him, in the name of Jesus, to get out of Mona because she was a Christian. Then Betty, kneeling with her face turned toward God said, "I discern a spirit of deception. Is that it, Mona?"

"Yes, yes. I've been deceived!" she cried as she rocked back and forth. With deep down groanings she grabbed her stomach, and then her throat—and gasped. Betty prayed, claiming the blood and name of Jesus; and the demon came out like something being wrenched from somebody.

The prison worker, still holding Mona's hand, looked up at her. "It didn't even look like the same person. She actually *glowed,*" she said. "Her facial muscles had relaxed, and she looked ten years younger. Such peace on her countenance."

We all threw our arms around each other and cried tears of joy and victory. Betty then volunteered to keep in touch with Mona as her friend and helper.

Victory! Don't worry about getting the perfect Scripture to resist Satan. Get a few well in hand and use them! Pick up your Sword of the Spirit, the Word of God, then practice wielding it against our arch enemy—Satan. There *is* victory!

How do we do spiritual warfare praying for each other? Once we have found the appropriate Scripture, is it enough just to quote it in a monotone to Satan? Oh no! Not only is *what* we pray important, but *how* we pray it makes a difference.

The Bible gives us many instructions as to *how* to pray for "the saints"—those who are at war with Satan because they already have been transferred out of his evil kingdom.

Not only does Ephesians 6:18 tell us to pray, it also gives us explicit guidelines of *how* Christians should pray for one another in the spiritual battle with Satan.

With all prayer and petition pray at all times in the Spirit, and with this in view, be on the alert with all perseverance and petition for all the saints (Ephesians 6:18).

"PRAYER"
First we must recognize that this verse is discussing actual *praying*. What is prayer? It is not just studying prayer or talking about prayer; it is *praying*.

Prayer is our means of involving the omnipotent God of the universe in our personal spiritual battle with Satan. Prayerlessness actually is arrogantly saying that we do not need

God. Even the disciples, watching Jesus' deep prayer life, asked Him to teach them to pray.

Prayer is the *power* for the spiritual battle with Satan. It utilizes the power of the armor-giver, God. So, *how* can we make sure our prayers are effective enough to transfer God's power in heaven to His children down here on earth? Here are some of the "how to's" for effective prayer.

Prayer in Ephesians 6:18-20—both defensive praying for each other (verse 18) and offensive praying for the lost (verses 19-20)—is part of God's armor (see chapter 5).

But this prayer comes *after* the Christian has put on the other pieces of the armor of God. As long as Christians are clothing themselves with Satan's sinful lifestyle, we will be not only defenseless but powerless in prayer. (See 1 John 3:22.) So spiritual warfare praying is for those who have taken off Satan's garb of sin and are fully clothed with God's holy armor.

"PRAYER AND PETITION"

The word "prayer" means praying in general and is the most frequently used word about praying in the Bible. It includes praise, adoration, confession, asking, etc. All of these should be included in our spiritual warfare praying.

However, the word "petition" is more specific. It means praying for a *specific need*. It involves *asking* for something. This Greek word "deesis" frequently is translated "supplication," and both it and "prayer" are often used together. So it is more than general praying. *"Petition" is specifically asking God to grant our requests for specific needs*. Petitions are extremely important in spiritual warfare praying.

The needs of Christians in our spiritual warfare are varied. They can be mental, physical, emotional, or spiritual. A woman brought a special need to me in West Germany last fall.

At the Protestant Women of the Chapel convention, Janie (not her real name) asked to speak to me alone. She trembled slightly as she said, "We are in a successful ministry of helping addicts get delivered from drugs, alcohol, etc. I myself have been delivered from them, but I still have another problem. No matter how much I pray, I still can't give up cigarettes. I've struggled and struggled, giving them up over and over—only to be right back smoking again." She dropped her head as she pleaded, "Can you please help me?"

Feeling angry at Satan for keeping this Christian in his clutches so tightly, I addressed him forcefully. "Satan, you have no right to do this to Janie. She belongs to Jesus. He is living in her. And the Bible says that He that is in her is greater than you are, so you must leave. In the name of Jesus, the blood of Jesus is flowing against you. Satan, get out!" At the end of the week, she came to me beaming, "I haven't had a cigarette all week!"

Paul admitted his needs because he knew the importance of prayer in the spiritual battle he was fighting continuously. Writing of his extreme affliction, so that he even despaired of life, Paul gave credit for his delivery to God—*through the prayers of many people.*

> You also join in helping us through your prayers, that thanks may be given by many persons on our behalf for the favor bestowed upon us through the prayers of many (2 Corinthians 1:11).

Paul knew the formula for getting people to petition God for his needs: (1) *admit* your need, and (2) *ask* people to pray. It is much easier to pray for somebody else than admit our own needs, but Paul wasn't too proud to admit and ask. Even after his direct encounter with the risen Jesus on the Damascus Road, he didn't have an "I can do it myself" attitude. No, he depended on the prayers of other believers and humbled himself enough to ask.

In his Ephesians 6 spiritual warfare section, Paul admitted a specific need in his spiritual battle for souls. He asked other believers to pray for him to have boldness in making known the mystery of the Gospel.

I learned twenty-five years ago to admit my needs and ask for prayer. My 24-Hour Prayer Clock, board, prayer calendar, and telephone prayer chain all faithfully pray for my ministry and my family—because I ask.

While I was writing chapter 9 on praying for each other for this book, I suddenly could not go on. After working a couple of weeks on it, I felt a blanket of confusion settle on my mind. Unbelievable interruptions kept my mind in a state of wondering where I was. (That is the only place Satan attacked me directly while writing this book. So I'm wondering if my writing about how to use Scripture against Satan when praying for each other threatens him the most.)

I had outlined the main points and was putting illustrations in when suddenly the whole thing became a jumble. After twenty-five years of actively battling Satan in a prayer ministry, the pile of illustrations I had pulled from my material was a couple of inches deep. I leafed through, reshuffled, and rewrote until my mind was swimming. A hopelessness of ever making sense of the stack gripped me. I called my prayer chains over and over, but Satan hung on tenaciously. He would not give up—until in desperation I just put it aside and turned my attention to a different chapter. (By the way, I wrote that chapter without any confusion.)

After Christmas I settled in once again to write chapter 9. At a Board Meeting I explained to my members the confusion I had felt before, and I asked for special prayer. They really got down to business against Satan in prayer. Then I dug out that chapter of my manuscript and read what I had written. I had thought it was a confused mess. To my amazement, a large part of the chapter already was clearly and concisely typed. It was not unusable material. The problem had been Satan's confusion and deceit—in me.

In our spiritual battle, all Christians need other Christians to pray for their specific needs, because we all have them.

"ALL PRAYER AND PETITION"

"All" is another qualifier for our spiritual warfare prayers of Ephesians 6:18. This means that *all kinds* of prayer—public, private, secret, formal, and spontaneous—should be made for all saints.

My speaking tour in Central America in the spring of 1989 (referred to in chapter 10) is a wonderful example for all kinds of prayer—some organized, some spontaneous, some private, some in groups. I continuously felt the power of those prayers in the frequent satanic hasslings on that trip.

In Guatemala City someone broke into the pastor's study just a few feet from where I was speaking in the next room. It was just minutes after I had brought my purse and brief-case from there and put it by my feet on the platform, and they had just locked up the offering in a desk drawer in that study. Then that night, the alarm system in the car in which I had arrived went off right outside the window closest to where I was speaking. So the Women's Aglow group formed a prayer chain to pray continuously for my safety while I went to El Salvador for meetings the next day.

After completing my five-day speaking series in one country, many women spontaneously stayed after the last meeting. They prayed for my traveling companion Bea's and my safety as we went into a strife-torn neighboring country.

Also, my friend Betty from Florida always has had a letter waiting for me in every overseas destination where I go to minister—telling me exactly what she is praying for me that day. Her letters were there in Central America—encouraging me, and (much more importantly) releasing God's power!

When I returned from Central America, I wiped away tears at my Board Meeting as my members recounted their incredible prayer support for me while I was in Guatemala, El Salvador, and Costa Rica. Esther came over to my chair and hugged me as tears welled up in her eyes. "I'm so glad you're home. God has been waking me over and over, night after night to pray for you." Then she sighed, "I'm exhausted!" Others told how God had stopped them many, many times each day, telling them to "pray for Evelyn." And then they told me how they did.

My 24-Hour Prayer Clock kept up unbroken praying all during that trip, petitioning the Father night and day for me.

Also the daily intercessors on our Prayer Calendar, who fight the spiritual battles for our ministry in prayer year in and year out, prayed about all my flights, traveling, and speaking for each day. These prayed especially about my fatigue, knowing that things would be added to my already too-full itinerary. Many mornings we got up at 4:15, took a plane, spoke all day and evening, slept as little as 4 hours, and got up again. When I returned home, my husband said, "You don't even have jet lag!" And I didn't.

One of the most wonderful results of all that prayer was Satan was not able to fill our meeting places with his evil presence. God's presence was the strongest I've ever felt at any meeting. Many people mentioned that they could absolutely *feel* God filling the room.

With people being abducted in the taxi right in front of our car, with guerillas knocking out all the electricity and infiltrating our meeting, with bombs exploding in cars on the street where I was speaking, and not being allowed to leave on my scheduled and ticketed flight—I had needs, specific needs! I know I was a threat to Satan as I continuously told Christians and non-Christians alike that the only answer to their problems was Jesus. But prayer kept Satan powerless.

When I wrote my thank-you letter to my pray-ers, I said, "God truly 'does come in proportion to our need.' But He also 'comes in proportion to your prayer!' "

Perhaps these many different kinds of prayer will help you as you seek to find different ways of praying for the spiritual needs of those you support.

PRAY "AT ALL TIMES"
Praying at all times means that spiritual warfare praying is more than our usual spasmodic personal praying, Sunday morning "prayer moment for missionaries" in church, or even our regularly scheduled prayer meetings.

Praying at all times means that the *attitude* of the believer's mind is to be one of perpetual prayer. That is what Paul meant when he said we are to "pray without ceasing" in 1 Thessalonians 5:17.

Paul asked those in Colossae to petition God for his needs while they were *devoting* themselves to prayer.

Devote yourselves to prayer, keeping alert in it with an attitude of thanksgiving; praying at the same time for us as well (Colossians 4:2-3).

After sharing about prayer possibilities for them at a missionary field council, one missionary wistfully said to me, "Oh, I wish *I* had prayer like that!"

"PRAY IN THE SPIRIT"
This requirement in Ephesians 6 for powerful spiritual warfare praying is confusing to some. It is even shunned by others not wanting to do anything "weird." Some associate it only with biblical speaking in tongues. So what does "in the Spirit" in Ephesians 6:18 really mean?

Whereas the Father and the Son are in heaven, the Holy Spirit is *with* and *in* the believer. (See John 14:16-17.) Prayer is a cooperation between God and the believer. It is presented to the Father, in the name of the Son, and inspired and prayed by the Holy Spirit. It is the Holy Spirit's part of the effectual prayer process—from within ourselves.

But it is more simple to explain than to practice experientially. For many, many years the Holy Spirit has been an intricate part of my personal prayer life. A certain inexplainable—but definitely recognizable—thing happens when I consciously converse with, wait for, and receive power from the Holy Spirit while I pray. It is sweet, powerful, and exhilarating, yet awesome and humbling.

This praying in the Spirit most likely is what John experienced when he received his breathtaking revelation of Jesus recorded in the first chapter of Revelation: "I was *in the Spirit* on the Lord's Day" (Revelation 1:10, italics added).

It doesn't say there was anything unusual about John being "in the Spirit" on the Lord's Day, nor should it be unusual for us. We have the same Holy Spirit living within us that John had, though I'm sure we have not practiced and developed this facet of prayer as he had.

A board member recently said to me, "Praying in the Spirit is what we experienced at our monthly board meetings. It is praying in one accord—with our spirits bearing witness that what we are praying is right. It is a confirmation from the Spirit in us, working among us."

Jude 20 tells us: "But you, beloved, building yourselves up on your most holy faith; *praying in the Holy Spirit.*"

Also, when we do not know *how* to pray, the Holy Spirit takes our feeble, well-meaning prayers to the Father in the throne room according to His will.

> And in the same way the Spirit also helps our weakness, for we do not know *how to pray* as we should, but the Spirit Himself intercedes ... for the saints according to the will of God (Romans 8:26-27, italics added).

So praying "in the Spirit" is not praying our own ideas, praying answers, telling God what to do, why to do it, and when to do it (as so much of our prayer is). It is being so in tune with the Holy Spirit, that we let—yes, *want*—Him to take our prayers to the Father according to God's will.

The whole triune Godhead is involved in the spiritual battle, and this is one of the Holy Spirit's most vital roles. It is His part in our praying.

"Be on the Alert"

This is a timely and needed admonition in our learning how to pray for each other in spiritual warfare from Ephesians 6:18.

The ultimate battle between the two kingdoms of Satan and Jesus was fought the weekend of the Garden of Gethsemene, the Cross and the Resurrection. Amazingly, it started in prayer—perhaps the deepest struggle planet earth ever has known as Jesus agonized in the Garden. Then came the unbelievable *lack of prayer* of His followers.

While Jesus was entering into the battle that would free the captives from Satan's kingdom, He not only sweat drops of blood himself as He prayed the final "God's will" in His life on earth, but He *expected* His disciples to be praying also. However, repeatedly returning to them, He found them

sleeping instead. Sharp rebuke and heartbreaking disappoint-
ment must have been mingled together in His words to
them: "What, could ye not watch with Me one hour? Watch
and pray, that ye enter not into temptation: the spirit indeed
is willing, but the flesh is weak" (Matthew 26:40-41, KJV).

Jesus continues to expect His followers to keep on *the alert*
and pray as we work together inviting Satan's captives into
Jesus' freedom. How do we do this?

First, we are to take life seriously and be aware that our
adversary actually is out there trying to devour us. And we
must be sharp-eyed, staying on the *alert* to that tactic of
Satan.

> Be of sober spirit, be on the alert. Your adversary the devil
> prowls about like a roaring lion, seeking someone to de-
> vour (1 Peter 5:8).

Also, Satan is a deceiver and a liar, so we must keep on the
alert to catch what we need to pray about for other believers.
And we even must be alert to the fact that they need our
prayers after we are aware of their need.

I praise God for Christians who really are on the *alert* for
me and who are willing to pray in my frequent attacks by
Satan.

The night before my prayer seminar in a wealthy Texas city
we met as usual for our Friday night committee prayer meeting. When the chairman arrived home there was a very weird
voice recorded on her telephone answering machine, though
she had not given her number anywhere for registrations.
Starting at the beep were the words "call home." Then "Is
Evelyn Christenson coming this weekend?" Long pause. "Is
she there now?" Another extended pause. "Thank you very
much!"

An uncanny fear engulfed her. Finding that no one had
called me from home, the chairman was very unnerved, in-
sisting I look thoroughly through the room while she kept
the phone line open. She then called the committee members
for special prayer, and assigned a pastor to be with me every

minute of the seminar the next day. (Later a board member with a ministry to local high school students in the occult said, "Evelyn, that's how the witches and warlocks work—fear.")

But Satan's fear did not get to me. Staunchly hanging on to 1 John 4:4, I went to sleep in Jesus' peace—while several prayed all night! And the Intercessory Prayer Ministry they formed in that church continues to send me reminders of what petitions they are praying specifically for me to this day!

Also, we should stay open to *God's alerting us to the needs of other saints* 24 hours a day.

I have a friend in Alabama who is very *alert* to God's telling her to pray. Her notes keep me advised of when God remarkably alerts her to my specific needs. One need was when our two daughters, their husbands and our four grand-daughters were nearly overcome with carbon monoxide gas in a Wisconsin cottage. A recent note said:

Dear Evelyn:
A while back I called you and told you that God had alerted me in my spirit to pray for a member of your family who was in danger. It was then that I learned your nephew had just been murdered.

The same intense call to prayer came on the eleventh at 3:30 in the morning. God woke me then to pray for your protection. At first I lay awake in bed praying for you, but then it became obvious to me that this was going to be a real battle and would take quite a lot of time and energy. So I slipped out of bed and came to the kitchen where I travailed in what I can only refer to as "warfare prayer." It was daylight before God released me to quit praying for you. I had real peace that you were safe and well.

It was good to talk to you on the thirteenth and hear for myself about your experience at that seminar."

The closing of the note said that what woke her to pray was seeing me (in her sleep) very plainly in a hotel room in grave danger.

The following incident was the one she was referring to, which God had alerted her to pray about for me. There was unusual concern for my safety when I arrived at the chairman's house in Oklahoma for the pre-seminar dinner and prayer meeting. The day before they had found a ring of blood around their whole house. The police said it was human blood and searched every local hospital and morgue for a victim. Not only did that committee multiply the intensity of their prayers for me that night, but had made a large 3 foot by 3 foot chart with a member signing up to pray for me every single hour from the discovery on Thursday through my arriving home by plane after the seminar.

We will not know until we get to heaven what dangers and disasters God has averted because somebody prayed!

Jesus knew keeping *alert* would not be easy. But He also knew the future and how vicious the battle with Satan would be. So He warned us in Luke 21:36: "But keep on the alert at all times, praying in order that you may have strength to escape all these things that are about to take place, and to stand before the Son of Man."

"PRAY WITH ALL PERSEVERANCE"
This is an important lesson in learning *how* we should pray for one another in our spiritual warfare from Ephesians 6:18. This is faithfulness and "stick-to-it-iveness" in prayer.

A woman phoned this morning asking us to help her pray for her Christian husband who had been gone—in Satan's clutches—living with another woman for thirteen months. "I've worn out every kind of prayer for him," she said. "But I'm still persisting in prayer!"

Jesus taught perseverance in prayer by telling His followers a parable about the persistent widow, "to show that at all times they ought to pray and not to lose heart" (Luke 18:1).

The 120 followers of Jesus, with His Gethsemane rebuke still stinging in their hearts, evidently had learned this lesson well. From the time Jesus ascended back to heaven until He sent the Holy Spirit ten days later at Pentecost—they continued steadfastly in prayer. And the Book of Acts reads almost like a "prayer log" of the baby church.

So often someone tells me they are tempted to quit pray-ing. They've been praying three months, three years, some-times even thirty years. But my answer always is, "Don't give up. We prayed for twenty-five years for my father to come to Jesus, and thirty for my brother to turn his life over to Jesus. And they both did."

Telephone prayer chains we helped organize over the last twenty years still are "persisting in prayer." One in California just sent me a birthday card telling me I was often remem-bered through their eleven years of faithful praying. The prayer chain we organized in 1968 in our "What Happens When Women Pray" church is still going, and the chairman wrote me about it just last week.

In Scotland in 1981, 650 people came to our prayer semi-nar in Glasgow, and 450 of them signed up to organize a national telephone prayer chain. Now that chain has spread all over the British Isles, and I felt privileged that they were still praying while I did my prayer tour there in 1989. Dur-ing this Glasgow prayer seminar, the power and presence of God just engulfed that Glasgow Civic Center because of all that persistent, faithful praying!

PRAYING FOR "ALL THE SAINTS"

This will produce the unity among *all* Christians which was the burden of Jesus' High Priestly Prayer in John 17. There is one real body of Jesus—not individual churches or denom-inations—but the universal body of Christ. It is made up of all the real believers, all those who have been transferred out of Satan's kingdom and into Jesus' kingdom.

All means not just professional ministers, evangelists, or missionaries. All of us need prayer in the spiritual battle.

We were having our first International Prayer Assembly in Seoul, Korea in 1984, with pray-ers from sixty-nine coun-tries. We were shocked when one official representative of a European country was aghast at our plans to make our call to prayer to "every Christian." Haughtily he said, "If I ask *my* people to pray with *them*, they won't pray at all!"

One of the most important parts of my prayer seminars is the rule we've enforced for many years. We ask that the steering committee be made up of representatives from all the churches of the community, if possible. And that they pray *together* for at least six months before the seminar. Such a fantastic unity develops among them, that many go on praying together after the seminar—or organize a community-wide telephone prayer chain.

If we are going to be successful in our battle against Satan, we cannot spend our time fighting each other!

There are many other principles necessary for effective spiritual warfare praying in the Bible.

"In Faith" is part of how to resist Satan when he seeks to devour us like a roaring lion from 1 Peter 5:8-9.

But resist him, firm in your faith (verse 9).

A young wife came to me asking for help at a week-long convention. "I accepted Jesus four years ago," she explained. "Before that I had been deeply involved in the occult. But since I accepted Jesus, I have not been able to look in a mirror. I always see an image other than my own. It's awful," she shuddered.

My teeth clenched in determination as I started to pray for her. "Satan, you have no right to keep this Christian in bondage. I claim the blood of Jesus against you. Get out! You know Jesus defeated you once and for all on the cross. And He is living in her. In the name of Jesus—be gone!"

At the end of the week she came bouncing up to me. "I've been looking at myself in the mirror all week," she grinned.

It is extremely important not to waver in spiritual warfare praying. It must be a stubborn stand against Satan.

"Fervently" describes the kind of prayer prayed for Peter when he was kept in prison by Herod. The Apostle James had just been put to death by Herod, so the Christians had gathered together to pray for Peter. (We are not told anything about their praying for James before he was killed.)

Peter was bound with two chains, sleeping between two

soldiers and with guards at the door when God sent an angel to deliver him supernaturally from that prison—while they prayed for him.

Our battle with Satan also is supernatural. Our lukewarm, halfhearted prayers don't do much to loosen Satan's hold. But, "The effectual *fervent* prayer of a righteous man availeth much!" (James 5:16, KJV italics added)

"Beseech" Jesus used the word *beseech* in asking us to pray for one another in the spiritual battle. But, surprisingly, He wanted us to pray, not for protection or safety, but for others of us to go out into His harvest: "The harvest is plentiful, but the laborers are few; therefore *beseech* the Lord of the Harvest to send out laborers into His harvest" (Luke 10:2, italics added).

Harvest of what? *People still captive in Satan's kingdom!* God's harvest is lost souls!

Beseech means more than just "to pray." It involves "to desire, to long for." *Beseeching* is wrestling, agonizing, weeping in prayer. It is the kind of praying we do when we really see as eternally lost all those who don't believe in Jesus.

All defensive prayers for each other are *so that* we can wage an effective, powerful, and uninhibited offensive attack against Satan and his kingdom of darkness. Praying for each other is not just to make us safe from Satan's fiery darts, but it is in order that we may be able to launch our offensive warfare for the souls held captive in Satan's kingdom.

One of the members of our denominations' Prayer Commission has just returned to her field of missionary service in Africa. "What *didn't* you learn in your Bible school and seminary training about prayer that you needed when you got to a foreign country?" I asked.

"About *spiritual warfare*," she answered immediately. "We never were taught that it even existed, much less how to recognize, cope with—and especially how to pray for it—and each other in it."

So, all the instructions as to *how* to pray for each other in our spiritual battle with Satan are in the Bible. All we need to do is use them.

Jesus knows Satan will do everything in his power to keep Christians from working with Him to rescue people out of Satan's evil kingdom. He will use any diabolical tactic necessary to *sift* us in order to render us ineffective in our battle for souls.

So, in addition to all those wonderful people praying for us, we have a source of prayer for us that is not human. *Jesus, the very Son of God, also is praying up in heaven while we fight our battle with Satan down here on earth.*

Jesus is praying because He knows we are just as vulnerable to Satan's attacks as His disciple Peter was. He knows Satan is sifting His followers today—just as much as Peter.

What is "sifting"? It is those difficulties caused by Satan to rob Christians of their power and effectiveness in their work for Jesus. Those problems Satan brings that make us useless in our battling him for souls for Jesus.

PETER'S SIFTING

Peter was about to become the spokesman for the new church Jesus left on earth to launch the Gospel into the whole world, so Satan became very nervous and decided to nip it in the bud. He evidently worried enough to get drastic—drastic enough to shake Peter violently like the sifting of wheat.

Just before Jesus was betrayed by Judas and denied by Peter, He told Peter these very sobering words: "Simon, Simon," Jesus said, "Satan has demanded permission to *sift you like wheat*" (Luke 22:31, italics added).

From whom did Satan demand such a diabolical thing? It must have been from God, for no other would have had the right to grant that kind of a request to a supernatural being regarding a true follower of Jesus. And obviously, judging from Peter's fall, Satan was granted that permission.

I tried to imagine how a grain of wheat in Jesus' day *felt* while it was being sifted. Being violently shaken, tumbling out of control through other wheat, thrown unmercifully from side to side in the container while its outer coat was being torn from its kernel—its very self. Sifted!

BUT JESUS HAD PRAYED

Jesus knew ahead of time not only that Satan was going to attack Peter, but also that Peter was going to fall when sifted by Satan. So, even before warning Peter about the temptation, Jesus already *had* prayed. And Jesus hastened to add these fantastic words to Peter, "But I have prayed for you" (Luke 22:32).

We are not told the content of very many of Jesus' prayers while here on earth. What He prayed in those lonely places or on those all night prayer trysts with His Father are not known to us. But this is one time Jesus told Peter exactly what He had prayed for him: "that your faith may not fail; and you, when you have turned again, strengthen your brothers" (verse 32).

So we know that at least some of the time when Jesus was praying, *it was for His followers in their spiritual battle with Satan.*

But the content of Jesus' prayer is frightening. Jesus knew He had to pray that when Peter *did* fall—his *faith would not fail.*

Then bold, impetuous Peter vehemently denied such an unthinkable possibility, declaring he was ready to go to prison and even death with Jesus! But Jesus, knowing all things, sadly stated, "I say to you, Peter, the cock will not crow today until you have denied three times that you know Me" (verse 34).

And the day was not over before cowardly Peter not only denied Jesus after His arrest, but even declared he didn't know what they were talking about. "And immediately, while we was still speaking, a cock crowed!"

Satan had temporarily won. His tactic of sifting Peter to keep him from spearheading the spread of the Gospel which would release captives from his evil kingdom had worked. Peter was useless to Jesus in that state.

TODAY'S SIFTING

There are many different ways that Satan sifts Christians today. Some methods are drastic; some are seemingly mild.

I was horribly jolted by yesterday's mail as I opened a document about a pastor friend of mine who had been an unusual threat to Satan and who had succumbed to Satan's sifting. He had found Jesus as His Saviour, escaping from a childhood home of satanic occult power controlling and empowering the evil supernatural professional lives of his whole family. Scenes of his parents conducting seances, trumpets flying through the air, and keys bending in locks without a human hand holding them were all too familiar to him.

Satan must have been devastated as this man had become an evangelical preacher. Imagine Satan's extreme nervousness when he not only exposed these Satan-empowered goings on, but actively taught and practiced the power of Jesus' Name and His blood against those things in his Christian ministry.

Satan's subtle sifting started slowly, unnoticed at first. However, it soon became obvious to some of us that Satan was getting a toehold on him personally. We tried to warn him; but he, like Peter, felt he was immune to Satan's tactics and sifting. He would never fall, he told us smugly at first. Then his smugness turned to defiance as he ignored all signs of Satan's sifting.

But fall he did. The many young women who followed his

ministry turned his head—until one particular one came into his life. He eventually ran off with her, leaving his wife and children. They lived as "father and daughter" in a house while together they started a "ministry" in another state.

It was a copy of his death certificate that came in my mail yesterday, listing him as "widowed." He had left strict orders for his obituary not to appear in any newspaper, and his death certificate to be kept secret. But somehow a copy of it got to his very much alive wife and children—and to me. I cringed as I read his dying instructions that his "daughter" was to screen all the requests for the tape of his funeral. And his last wish to her was, "Secure my body in the grave well, as the satanists will want to take my body and use it for satanic rituals."

Sifted by Satan!

EXPECT SIFTING

We are a threat to Satan when we try to rescue his captives from his kingdom. We also should *expect Satan's sifting*. He will try every tactic possible to hinder, thwart, and make ineffective our efforts to rescue captives out of his evil kingdom.

How does "sifting like wheat" feel to us today? Like the little grain in Jesus day, we are violently tossed until it is impossible to keep our feet on the ground, flung mercilessly at the will of Satan.

I have gone through many such siftings in my life, and I know that that is how one feels. There is no question in my mind that Satan, for some reason, feels I need to be stopped in my tracks like Peter. Have you felt it too?

But Satan's sifting is not always that easy to identify. Frequently his siftings are the ordinary irritations which unnerve us, disrupt our ministry for Jesus, or keep our minds occupied just trying to survive financially, physically, or emotionally—making us ineffective in our battle against him.

Occasionally, when our ministry for Jesus is especially threatening to Satan, he will sift with some, or many, earth-shattering events. But even then, it sometimes is hard to identify the *source* of the bad things that are happening to us. And even harder to catch *why*.

We must realize that the more earnest and the more effective we become in helping lost people get transferred out of Satan's diabolical kingdom, the more nervous Satan will become. And the more nervous, the more he will concentrate his activities on sifting us. And the more he sifts us, the harder it becomes to keep effective in our winning souls out of his kingdom of darkness into Jesus' kingdom.

JESUS PRAYS TODAY

If Jesus knew He had to pray for Peter's sifting in that day, doesn't He know Satan also is determined to sift us today? Doesn't Jesus know Satan is just as nervous about our invading his kingdom here and his strongholds in foreign pagan lands with the Gospel of Jesus? So, isn't it just as logical that Jesus also is praying the same prayer for us right now?

Yes, Jesus is still praying for today's Peters—us, His laborers. He still is interceding today for us—always—at the right hand of the Father.

> Hence, also, He [Jesus] is able to save forever those who draw near to God through Him, since *He always lives to make intercession for them* (Hebrews 7:25, italics added).

But the praying Jesus of today isn't trudging dusty paths and climbing inhospitable mountains to find a place of prayer. No, He is described in the very next verse as "*a high priest, holy, innocent, undefiled, separated from sinners and exalted above the heavens*" (7:26, italics added).

Our Jesus isn't just a human being struggling in a corrupt human body up there in heaven. No, He is the One God has highly exalted. He's the One with that name which is above every name—to which every knee should bow, of those who are in heaven and on earth, and under the earth. He's the One every tongue should confess is Lord, to the glory of God the Father. (See Philippians 2:9-11.) That is who our intercessor in heaven is today!

Jesus. the One who can—and will—keep our faith from failing when Satan sifts us!

Early this morning I was lying in bed just communing with my Lord before rising. There had been a long period of unusually hard circumstances with one of my board member's finances for which I had wrestled in prayer for several months. As I started to labor again in prayer for them, suddenly tears sprang up in my eyes as sweeping over me was the thought, "Jesus is praying for me!"

I cried softly in that pre-dawn blackness. Tears of joy and tears of relief and tears of assurance all mingled together. "Oh, Jesus, I love You!" My heart almost burst in my chest as I stayed, silent in His presence—*being prayed for by my Jesus!*

TIME TO THANK AND PRAISE

But I also was thanking God for Satan's attacks on me and on my board, because that means Satan is nervous about our winning souls into Jesus' kingdom. What we are doing is important enough to get the attention and hassling from Satan.

It was just the day before that I had prayed over the phone *with* that board member and her husband on a particularly dark day. And I had thanked God that Satan was nervous enough to sift them because of *their own effectiveness for Jesus.* I thanked God for what He was going to do with these two dynamic Christian leaders, like Peter, after Satan got done with their sifting.

Back in the 1970s, my United Prayer Ministries board became aware of a pattern emerging. Satan frequently hassled many or all of our members and their families at the same time. Then, as we kept track through the years, we noticed another pattern. It always was when God had just expanded our ministry or was about to open a new door in our ministry with a new book, new tape series, another continent on which to minister, or a new radio broadcast language that Satan sprang into action. So it was then I said to those prayers on my board, *"This is the time to praise!"* I taught them it was the time to thank God—that our ministry for Jesus was effective enough to make Satan nervous enough to spend his time trying to disrupt it?

When your hassles are undeserved and seem to be from Satan, have you learned to thank God that what you are doing for Jesus is important enough to cause Satan to try to disrupt you?

THAT YOUR FAITH WILL NOT FAIL

I closed that phone prayer with my board member and her husband by encouraging them to have faith. Faith—not in other people, not in what they could do in their own strength, not in financial security—but faith in God.

"No matter what," I said just before I hung up the phone, "hang on *in faith* to *who God is!*"

Sometimes in our sifting by Satan, it seems we have nothing left to cling to. People betray us, all attempts at straightening out our problems seem to fail, and even our own strength melts like warm wax as our knees buckle under us. It is then we almost wonder if God too has deserted us.

Many, many times through the years all I had to hang on to as Satan pulled the rug out from under me—was faith. Not fleshed out with padding of the security of others or circumstances, but just the bare bones of faith.

It was a year and a half ago when, everything seemed so hopeless in a family situation, that God said to me, "Faith!" As I write, the solution is not here yet, and sometimes my faith falters a little as I wonder at God's slowness in answering all our prayers. But whenever I feel myself wavering just the least little bit, God firmly reminds me, "Have faith, Evelyn!"

It is in times like these that God is the only thing to which we can cling. The only One who does care, and who has power enough to keep us from falling—and our faith from failing.

Now unto Him that is able to keep you from falling . . . (Jude 24, KJV).

But Peter did fall. He did succumb to Satan's sifting. Within hours of Jesus' warning to Peter, Judas had betrayed Jesus, starting the chain of events that would lead to the cross the next day. And when they arrested Jesus, Peter found himself sitting at the enemy's fire, vehemently denying His Lord—not once but three times—cursing and saying that he never knew Jesus.

The sifting was complete! That's why Jesus knew He had to pray that Peter's fall would not affect his deep-down faith. And it didn't. But it must have been possible for Peter's actual faith to fail or Jesus would not have bothered to pray that prayer for him.

It is very comforting to know that Jesus also knew that after Peter had fallen, he would turn again. Jesus said "*When* you have turned again"—not *if* you turn again. Then He gave Peter the job of strengthening his brothers after his return to Him. Jesus was assuring Peter in advance of his falling. I can almost hear Jesus thinking, "Just because you succumbed to Satan's sifting, Peter, doesn't mean you never will be of use to Me again."

Was Jesus preparing them all for the satanic sifting He knew would be heaped on His little band as they took the Gospel to the world? Was He teaching them one of the most-needed lessons they ever would learn, that *yes, you will be sifted,* and if you do fall, *there is a future of effectiveness for Me?*

ANOTHER PRAYER OF JESUS

It must have been hard for Jesus to leave that little band on earth to fend for themselves in the onslaught of Satan's inevitable sifting. So, before He left earth for heaven, He prayed a very important prayer for His disciples about Satan. In His great High Priestly prayer of John 17, Jesus prayed: "Father . . . I do not ask Thee to take them out of the world, but to keep them from the evil one" (John 17:15).

Jesus had told His followers that the world (Satan's domain) would hate them just as they hated Him. But, amazingly, Jesus did not pray for the Father to take them out of this hateful world, but only to deliver them from the source of their coming problems—Satan.

That word *from* actually means "out of the power of." So what Jesus actually prayed was, "Father, . . . I do not ask You to take them out of the world, but to keep them from the power of the evil one."

PRAYER FOR US TOO

Jesus added in that High Priestly Prayer these wonderful words for *us:* "I do not ask in behalf of these alone, but for those also who believe in Me through their word" (John 17:20).

We are some of those who have received and believed the Gospel from those disciples—passed on through almost two thousand years. And it is mind-boggling to think it was that long ago that Jesus, while still on earth, actually prayed for *us.* He prayed for us to be delivered out of the power of Satan, the evil one—when he sifts us.

And sift us he does!

OUR SIFTING

Peter was the one who preached the first sermon after Jesus rose from the dead and went back to heaven. And that sermon launched Jesus' church. So we can understand Satan's trying to stop Peter by sifting him *before* he had a chance to get started. He had to stop Peter before all those thousands of people in Satan's kingdom would accept Jesus, be transferred to Jesus' kingdom, and form the nucleus of Jesus' church on earth.

So today's pastors, priests, missionaries, Christian leaders, and lay people who are winning souls are particularly vulnerable to Satan's sifting, because they too are especially threatening to Satan in their roles of attacking his kingdom. Being a lay person or a professional on the offense against Satan almost invites Satan's fury. Whenever we are effectively working with Jesus to set people free from Satan's evil kingdom, we should not be surprised—but rather we should *expect sifting!*

INEVITABLE OUTCOME?

But was Peter's fall inevitable when Satan sifted him? Was it hopeless for Peter once he had been singled out as a target of Satan? Definitely not. Peter was the exception, not the norm. Though there are other examples in the Bible of a child of God falling when tempted, most did not. Yes, Judas betrayed Jesus after Satan "entered into him" and it was Satan who filled the hearts of Ananias and Sapphira to "lie to the Holy Spirit," but the Bible is filled with those like Job, the rest of the disciples, and Paul who—in spite of life-threatening siftings by Satan—*did not fall.*

Why? Because of God. God is omnipotent, and He has all the power that ever will be needed to keep His own from falling.

> Now unto Him that is able to keep you from falling, and to present you faultless before the presence of His glory with exceeding joy (Jude 24, KJV).

God also provides all the armor we ever will need for standing and withstanding in our battle with Satan—not even hinting at the possibility of falling in the Ephesians 6 spiritual warfare account.

And *God provides a way of escape* when we are tempted, so the outcome of Satan's sifting definitely does not have to be our falling. We are not doomed just because Satan decides we need hassling.

> No temptation has overtaken you but such as is common to man; and God is faithful, who will not allow you to be tempted beyond what you are able, but with the temptation will provide the way of escape also, that you may be able to endure it (1 Corinthians 10:13).

And, astoundingly, *God turns all our hard things, including Satan's siftings, into our good* because we love Him and are called according to His purpose. (See Romans 8:28.) Although Satan intends them for harm and destruction, God uses them to firm up our faith, teach us lessons, help others, make us more Christlike and equip us for future battles with Satan.

But, most importantly, falling from Satan's sifting is not inevitable—*because Jesus prays!* That is why Jesus prayed for us while He was here on earth—and still prays for us up in heaven. He knows and understands our battle with Satan's siftings on planet Earth.

It is very important to have other people praying for us. But the greatest privilege of all is to know that Jesus, *the very Son of God,* is bringing all our needs to the Heavenly Father *personally.* And when Satan tries to sift any one of us, it is the Jesus who defeated Satan on the cross and reigns eternally in heaven who prays. Jesus prays for us that we will not fall.

We are on the victory side!

J esus brought a new dimension of authority and power when He came to earth. Something changed between the Old and New Testaments. We now have Jesus' *name* and His *blood* with which to fight the spiritual battles against Satan both personally and for captives being rescued out of his evil kingdom. Jesus said to His followers; "Until now you have asked for nothing in My name; ask, and you will receive, that your joy may be made full" (John 16:24).

WHAT'S IN A NAME?

A name in Jesus' day meant all that a person was. When Jesus taught us in the Lord's Prayer to pray to the Father, "Hallowed be Thy name," He meant praying all that the Father is—who He is and what He has dedicated Himself to be. (See Matthew 6:9.)

So, Jesus' name includes all that He is too. Colossians 1:15-17 tells us clearly what Jesus is:

And He is the image of the invisible God, the firstborn of all creation. For by Him all things were created, both in the heavens and on earth, visible and invisible, whether thrones or dominions or rulers or authorities—all things have been created by Him and for Him. And He is before all things, and in Him all things hold together.

After Jesus' incarnation and death on the cross, God gave Jesus the name described in Philippians 2:9-11:

Therefore also God highly exalted Him, and bestowed on Him *the name which is above every name,* that at the name of Jesus every knee should bow, of those who are in heaven, and on earth, and under the earth, and that every tongue should confess that Jesus Christ is Lord, to the glory of God the Father (italics added).

Jesus' earthly father, Joseph, could not name his espoused wife's first Son. An angel of the Lord told him who and what Mary's Son by the Holy Spirit would be: "You shall call His *name Jesus,* for He will *save His people from their sins*" (Matthew 1:21.)

PRAYING IN JESUS' NAME

Jesus gave us a *new privilege* in prayer when He came to earth. We now can have access to the Father "in all that Jesus is." So when we pray in Jesus' name, we also are praying who He is, and what He has dedicated Himself to be. Only since His incarnation, death, resurrection, and ascension have God's children had this incredible dimension in prayer. *We now have a new power in prayer of asking in Jesus' name* that they did not have in Old Testament times. (See chapter 3 for all Jesus is.)

And whatever you ask *in My name,* that will I do, that the Father may be glorified in the Son (John 14:13, italics added).

More importantly, we not only have the privilege, but also the *authority* of Jesus' name in our spiritual warfare praying and battling against Satan.

In Aberdeen, Scotland, a lady asked me, "Do you remember me? I was the chairman of your seminar the last time you were here. I invited you to my house for tea because I had a problem with our daughter. She had gone to live with a gang practicing deep occult activities and was taking part in all the evil lifestyle with them. Her father and I were frantic, having tried everything to get her back home."

I assured her I remembered well, for we had had deep spiritual warfare prayer together for her daughter during that tea time. "But you had to leave right away," she continued, "so I asked you what I could do."

She reminded me that I had told her to get as many of her praying friends organized as possible to pray for her daughter—*claiming the blood and name of Jesus.* "I took your advice," she said, "and that very night even called praying friends in Bermuda, America, and the outer islands." That mother was absolutely radiant as she beamed, "And our daughter was delivered! And now she is working full time for Jesus!" The name and blood of Jesus really works.

WHAT AUTHORITY?

What kind of authority does Jesus' name include? Colossians 2:9-10 says it well:

> For in Him all the fullness of Deity dwells in bodily form, and in Him you have been made complete, and He is the *Head over all rule and authority.*

Whenever we see a "therefore" in the Bible, we look to see what it is "there for." The "therefore" in Jesus' Great Commission in Matthew 28:18-20 is very important. Jesus said that *because* "All authority has been given unto Me in heaven and on earth"—*therefore* "go and make disciples of all nations." So, it is because of Jesus' authority that we are to make disciples of all nations. This, of course, is rescuing them from Satan's kingdom into which they were born.

Also, *there is no other name that can transfer those who are captive in Satan's kingdom into Jesus' kingdom.* It is only those who receive Him and believe *in His name* that Jesus gave the right to become the Sons of God. (See John 1:12; 3:18; and 1 John 3:23.)

And there is salvation in no one else; for there is *no other name* under heaven that has been given among men, by which we must be saved (Acts 4:12, italics added).

There is no way Satan's name ever can compete with the authority of Jesus' name. According to Ephesians 1:21, Jesus is "far above all rule and authority and power and dominion, and *every name that is named* [including Satan's], not only in this age, but also in the one to come" (italics added).

WHY NOT THE NAME OF JESUS?

I kept track in a fine local church for five consecutive Sundays. The pastor preached eloquently out of the Old Testament (surely the Word of God). The choir sang great church anthems magnificently. But for those five Sunday mornings, not one person mentioned the name of Jesus—not even to close a prayer.

A close friend of mine is involved in reaching international students for Jesus in their city's university. "Evelyn," he said sadly, "I am playing racquetball regularly with my new friend from the Middle East so I can introduce him to Jesus. But I cannot take him to our church to hear about Jesus, because nobody mentions the name of Jesus in our services. Oh, everything is fine and biblical, but no different than he would hear from the Old Testament teachings in his mosque." They have been robbed of what we now have in Jesus!

The extreme of not using Jesus' name was shared at a California seminar interdenominational committee meeting. A member reported she was devastated because the board of her church had just forbidden their pastor to mention the name of Jesus on Sunday mornings. They didn't want to offend anybody.

There is a danger in Christians not using Jesus' name enough. After Jesus went back to heaven, He wrote letters through the Apostle John back to His churches on earth. He told the church at Ephesus all the good things about their church—their deeds, toil, perseverance, not enduring evil men, putting false prophets to the test, endurance, and not growing weary. But then He said, "But I have this against you, that you have left your first love. Remember therefore from where you have fallen, and repent and do the deeds you did at first."

In other words, "you have lost that first, exuberant love and exclusive preoccupation with *Me* you had at first." Then Jesus warned them that, if they didn't return to their first love, He would remove their church (lampstand). (See Revelation 2:1-5.) Is Jesus thinking the same thing about *your* church today?

NEW POWER IN MINISTRY

We now have a new power for our ministry—"in Jesus' name."

Just before writing this book as I was re-reading the book of Acts, I was overwhelmed how everything the apostles did after Jesus' ascension was "in the name of Jesus." The title given that accounting of the first years of the early church is "The Acts of the Apostles." But the more I read the more I knew I had to add my own words to that title: "The Acts of the Apostles—in the name of Jesus!"

For example, when Peter and John encountered a man who had been lame from his mother's womb who asked them for alms, Peter said, "I do not possess silver and gold, but what I do have I give to you: *In the name of Jesus Christ the Nazarene—walk!*" (Acts 3:6, italics added).

Then Peter, seizing him by the hand, raised him up. And with a leap he stood upright and began walking, leaping, and praising God! The power of the *name of Jesus!*

When all the people ran together full of amazement, Peter replied to them, "Men of Israel, why do you marvel at this, or why do you gaze at *us,* as if by our own power or piety we had made him walk?" (Acts 3:12, italics added) Then Peter, after saying that God had glorified His servant Jesus whom they had put to death, added, "And on the basis of faith *in*

His name, it is the *name of Jesus* which strengthened this man whom you see and know" (Acts 3:16, italics added).

(After God had moved greatly in our last Glasgow, Scotland seminar, I wrote in the margin of my Bible by those verses: "Do we think our piety and power brings the miracles in seminars? I *know* it isn't *my* power!")

Then the priests, the captain of the temple guard, and the Sadducees, disturbed by the teaching of Jesus, put Peter and John in jail until the next day. All who were of high-priestly descent questioned them the next day, asking, "By what power, or *in what name*, have you done this?" (Acts 4:7, italics added)

Peter unequivocally declared, "Let it be known to all of you, and to all the people of Israel, that *by the name of Jesus Christ the Nazarene* whom you crucified, whom God raised from the dead—*by this name* this man stands here before you in good health" (italics added).

Why did those leaders then command Peter and John *not* to speak or teach "in that name?" (Acts 4:18) Since they could not deny that a noteworthy miracle was apparent to all who lived in Jerusalem, they decided they had to stop this power of Jesus' name by commanding the apostles to stop using it. This, of course, only made them use that name with more confidence!

DEMONS CAST OUT IN JESUS' NAME

When the disciples were sent out two by two, they were given authority by Jesus to cast out demons. "And He was giving them power over the unclean spirits" (Mark 6:7). But it was not because of any human power or piety they possessed. Luke tells us that they returned with joy, saying, "Lord, even the demons are subject to us *in Your name!*" (Luke 10:17)

Jesus' great commission, given before ascending back to heaven, was not only for those followers of Jesus who were present, but is also for us. In Mark's recording of that commission, he included the dimension of going into all the world and preaching the Gospel in "Jesus' name."

And these signs will accompany those who have believed: *in My name* they will cast out demons (Mark 16:17, italics added).

The disciples of Jesus had solid basis believing these words of Jesus, for all through His earthly ministry they had watched Him have complete control over demons. They not only recognized Jesus as the Son of God and conversed with Him, but they immediately obeyed Jesus' every command. The demons even were terrified He would send them to the torment before their time. They knew He had complete authority to do with them as He chose.

In Capernaum even the onlookers were amazed, not only that Jesus' message was "with authority" (Luke 4:32), but that the demon possessing a man first identified Jesus as the Holy One of God—and then was cast out by Him. The crowd then began discussing with one another, "What is this message? For *with authority and power* He commands the unclean spirits, and they come out" (Luke 4:36, italics added).

We have the same Jesus they had while He was here on earth. But we too must be very careful never to try to wield power over Satan and his demons in our own strength or power. Satan, not us, will win. But with the authority of Jesus' name, they will be subject to us believers too.

Paul also knew his human limitations in dealing with the evil supernatural world. Once he was followed for many days by a slave-girl who was making much money for her masters by fortunetelling, because she had a *spirit of divination*. So, Paul used the authority of the name of Jesus.

But Paul was greatly annoyed, and turned and said *to the spirit,* "I command you *in the name of Jesus* Christ to come out of her!" And it came out at that very moment (Acts 16:18, italics added).

Many feel the ability to make money with paranormal power is just some highly cultivated human ability or a gift to special humans. Power for channeling, mental telepathy, and out of body experiences is sought after and usually highly respected today. But the Bible says that this girl's paranormal ability was due to an "it"—a "spirit of divination" in her. The "it" that came out was not a good power or even an evil influence; it was an evil spirit.

Is it possible that because we don't realize how much we need to use the "name of Jesus" today, we don't see the same kind of power in our churches as recorded in the Book of Acts? Our human plans, programs, and projects never will dislodge the hierarchy of the devil described in Ephesians 6:11-12. Only Jesus!

Colossians 3:17 says that whatever we do in word or deed, we are to do it *all in the name of the Lord Jesus*. Why? Because there is authority in that name—authority we can only have with the name of Jesus. Not our own name, the name of our church, our denomination or organization, but Jesus name!

I remember when my board member and her husband were devastated by unexplainable attacks on their daughter. She would shake, or her eyes would roll back, or she would become temporarily comatose, or wretch with dry heaves. Twice she tried to commit suicide with an overdose and inhaling lethal substances. She left a note to her siblings that Jesus loved them and she had to do this. Finally her mother cried out to Satan, "No! In the name of Jesus—you are not going to have her!"

Completely distraught, her father went to a pastor who had been saved out of a life of occult involvement. He asked if he was authorized to pray over his child for her deliverance. "Yes," the pastor answered, "it is very proper. You are her father." So in his simple way, that father claimed the blood of Christ, bound the spirits in the name of Jesus. And they came out! *In the name of Jesus!*

BLOOD OF JESUS
The other authority we have, in addition to Jesus' name, is Jesus' *blood*.

The power of His blood came when Jesus shed His blood

on the cross. Jesus appeared on earth for just one reason: to destroy the works of the devil. (See 1 John 3:8.) And at His death on the cross Jesus unequivocally defeated Satan, once for all. Satan knows this and realizes he cannot stand up against the blood of Jesus. Satan knows the blood of Jesus is the ultimate irresistible force in the universe against him.

So again, it is not through our own power—but the power of the blood of Jesus—that we are victorious over Satan and his kingdom. Revelation 12:9-11 clearly tells us of the authority of believers *through the blood of the Lamb, Jesus.*

And the great dragon was thrown down, the serpent of old who is called the devil and Satan, who deceives the whole world was thrown down to earth, and his angels were thrown down with him. And I heard a loud voice in heaven saying, "Now the salvation, and the power, and the kingdom of our God and the authority of His Christ have come . . . and they overcame him *because of the blood of the Lamb* and because of the word of the testimony (italics added).

Many of our problems in life are hassles from Satan. When they are, the blood of Jesus has power over them.

One day my daughter phoned saying, "Mother, I don't know what to do with our child. For several days she has seemed just the opposite of her usual personality. No matter what we do, nothing seems to help. We've tried extra love, but she obstinately rejects it completely. We've tried sending her to her room, but she gets angry and throws things. When we discipline her, she throws a tantrum. Please pray, Mother!"

As I was praying, a light suddenly dawned. God reminded me that this little one was being unduly influenced by Satan. My grandmotherly defenses went up, and I claimed the blood of Jesus over my little granddaughter. "Satan," I snapped at him, "you have *no right* to do this. She has Jesus in her heart and belongs to Him. *I claim the blood of Jesus against you. In His name—get out—right now!*"

A couple of days later when talking to my daughter, she said, "By the way, Mother, what did you pray for our daughter?" When I asked why, she said, "Something just seemed to snap. She was in her room alone, rebelling against the world, when suddenly she came down to the kitchen all smiles. Completely changed, she asked if she could please set the table for dinner. And she has been sweet as pie ever since. What *did* you pray, Mother?"

"I just claimed the *blood* of Jesus over her—and told Satan, *in the name of Jesus,* to get out."

Sometimes it is more than just a hassle from Satan, and authority must be taken over his actual demons.

Though there are many fine experts in the field of dealing with demons, any of us as believers can find ourselves confronted by someone needing our help. It is wise to seek professional help in severe cases, but we desperately need to be able to recognize when it is a demon and be able to use the authority Jesus gave to all of us.

At my seminar last fall the host pastor told me, "I was sound asleep one night last week when my doorbell rang. I stumbled out of bed in that stupor just after going to sleep. When I opened the door a teenage boy stood there. (That was not a surprise to me as I had had a large inner-city youth ministry.) But when he saw me, the pastor, his eyes rolled back in his head, he began frothing at the mouth, and becoming violent."

The pastor said he cried in desperation, "Oh, Lord, I can't even think in this sleepy stupor. What should I do?" Then he told me, "Immediately hitting my mind was 'Claim the blood of Jesus.' So I said, 'Demons, name yourselves.' Two immediately did—in horrible, unhuman voices. Then I just said, *'I claim the blood of Jesus against you. In the name of Jesus—get out!'* The boy immediately fell limp on the floor—and was free. The demons were gone."

HALLOWEEN

Then there are those drastic displays of Satan's power that we need to be able to handle. We should be aware that there are special days of the year when these things are more apt to take place than others. Satan's kingdom has its special days just as well as any other religion, including Halloween, spring and fall solstice, Christmas Eve, and Holy Week before Easter.

When I wrote the topics for the European Protestant Women of the Chapel's training week in West Germany, I didn't realize that the second day would be Halloween. (The chaplain in charge later told me that the occult was very prevalent in Western Europe. He described how witches had cursed him—and the chapel on the U.S. military base.)

While teaching on their "Shepherd" topic, we were contrasting the Old Testament shepherd and the New Testament shepherd—Jesus. On Halloween night I blissfully taught the material I had prepared on "What Is Unique about the New Testament Shepherd's Dying?" I explained that the New Testament Shepherd, Jesus, was the only shepherd ever to have the power to take up His own life again after being killed.

That night's teaching included such Satan-threatening points as: "Satan caused the incarnation of Jesus by bringing sin to planet earth"; "Jesus died to defeat the works of the devil" (1 John 3:8); "He rendered powerless him who had the power of death, that is, the devil" (Hebrews 2:14); and "Because Jesus took up His life again, His followers have—forgiveness of sins, redemption, transferred kingdoms, abundant life, eternal life, and the power of Jesus' blood over their enemy Satan."

At the close of the meeting there was thunderous applause when I emphasized, "He is Lord!" We sang to the top of our voices, "He is Lord, He is Lord; He is risen from the dead and He is Lord!" Then, in their small groups, they exploded in prayer as we thanked Jesus and praised Him for laying down His life for us. Next we thanked Him for shedding His blood—for us to have redemption and power.

After singing a song about *the blood of Jesus,* I asked those who were not absolutely sure they had this Shepherd Jesus as their personal Saviour and Lord to pray, and they prayed all over the whole room. While everyone praised God, an oriental woman sitting close to my husband loudly praised God, either in her native language or in tongues, for the victory.

But when I assigned the last prayer topic, we were in for a shock. "This is Halloween," I said. "This is the night the witches, warlocks, and their followers are celebrating their main night of the year. We are going to practice claiming the power of the blood of Jesus. I want each of you to think of something—such as your neighborhood, home, chapel building on your own military base—or someone such as your chaplain, pastor, or child. Now pray for their protection, *claiming the blood of Jesus—in the name of Jesus.*"

Positive praying swelled throughout the room—until the oriental woman suddenly arched her back, bared her teeth slightly, and again raised her voice above all the hundreds praying. But her praying changed. It was different, eerie. Fear engulfed many. The tone in the whole room changed. Many reported later feeling a cold chill—some across their feet, some down their backs. The room was in chaos, evil chaos.

I hesitated for a moment, but knew I had to take charge. So I stepped to the microphone, raised my voice above the din, and said, "Satan, I *claim the blood of Jesus over you.*" Then I prayed, "Father, we thank You that Jesus defeated Satan. And on this Halloween night *we are claiming victory in the name of Jesus.* He is Lord!" And they erupted in applause to Jesus.

The people returned to their rooms, scouring their Bibles for their authority over and protection from Satan. Some prayed into the night.

I was concerned that Satan had succeeded in disrupting our beautiful convention. But the next morning, we were in for a wonderful shock. After the lesson on how we hear the voice of the Shepherd today when we read the Bible, I sent them out to read Jesus' words in John 14 until they felt He was saying something to them personally. When they gathered in their discussion groups to share what He had said, almost everyone there—representing military bases from Iceland to Turkey—was stopped on the same verse: John 14:1

"Let not your heart be troubled; believe in God, believe also in *Me*" (italics added).

Victory, tears, hugs! They had their answer. Jesus!

Little did I know how much we would need what the song leader and I had done that afternoon. When we realized that it was Halloween, one of the most important holidays for witches and those in occult and Satan worship, we took some preventive action. The song leader and I walked through that large auditorium and, as we touched each chair, said, "In the name and blood of Jesus." And there was victory—but not without a battle—*in that blood and name!*

Last Halloween our daughter's church gave their children something more than a party instead of trick-or-treating out on the streets. While the children were partying—and learn ing about the real meaning of Halloween, their parents gath- ered in their prayer room. They prayed against the evil pow- ers so strongly at work that night in their community and our nation. They prayed for protection *in the power of the blood and the name of Jesus!*

WHAT ARE WE MISSING?

A song leader in a local church decided perhaps they shouldn't sing any songs about the blood of Jesus because blood could frighten the children. (At the same time a national study found that violence and killings on TV those children watch had just almost doubled.)

But it all depends on your point of view of that blood. As a child, one of our church's very favorite songs was, "There's Power in the Blood." Our song leader frequently would say, "Let's sing the word 'power' four times instead of two in the chorus." Then he would smile victoriously and pump his arm vigorously while we sang at the top of our lungs, "There is power, power, power, power, wonder working power—in the precious blood of the Lamb!"

The word most often used to describe Jesus' blood when I was a child was "precious." We closed our prayers, both public and private, with that word too. There was a reverent awe and deep love all rolled into one as we would pause deliberately on, "In the *precious* name of Jesus. Amen."

When attending a seminar series by Dr. Kurt Koch on the occult in the early 1970s, he emphasized over and over, "Be sure to sing lots of songs and read lots of Scripture containing the *blood of Jesus*. It's the power!"

And I remember staying in a pastor's home the night he and his wife had called in another pastor to pray over his wife. Since an unusual rebellion against God years before, she had been plagued with debilitating oppression and problems. All through that pastor's delivering her, he would have us read verse after verse from the Bible containing references to *Jesus' blood*. And then would have us sing song after song about victory in *Jesus' blood*. Not really understanding why, I obeyed. (Now I know.) Today that pastor's wife is the dynamic national head of a prayer movement in her whole denomination.

Sing praises to Jesus. Sing songs about His powerful blood. Sing "in the name of Jesus." Satan can't stand it. He'll have to flee!

WHY IS SATAN SO WORRIED ABOUT THE BLOOD?

Why shouldn't he be? After all, it was Jesus' blood that released us from the sins that Satan brought to earth. It was Jesus' blood that absolutely, unequivocally destroyed everything Satan has done and is striving to accomplish on earth. Just listen to what Jesus' blood did for believers against Satan:

- And *released us from our sins* by His blood (Revelation 1:5, italics added).

- Much more then, having now been *justified* by His blood, we shall be *saved from the wrath of God* through Him (Romans 5:9, italics added).

- Knowing that you were not *redeemed* with perishable things like silver and gold from your futile way of life inherited from your forefathers, but with precious blood, as of a lamb unblemished and spotless, the blood of Christ (1 Peter 1:18-19, italics added).

- In Him we have *redemption* through His blood, the *forgive-*

ness of our trespasses (Ephesians 1:7, italics added).

● And in the same way He took the cup after they had eaten [at the last supper], saying, "This cup which is poured out for you is the *new covenant in My blood*" (Luke 22:20, italics added).

We were not the only ones released from sins, justified, redeemed, forgiven, and transferred out of Satan's kingdom because of the blood of Jesus. His blood was for people of the whole world. Revelation 5:8-9 tells us the four living creatures and the twenty-four elders fell down before the Lamb (Jesus). And they sang a new song, saying: "Worthy art Thou to take the book, and to break its seals; for Thou wast slain, and didst purchase for God *with Thy blood* men from *every tribe and tongue and people and nation*" (italics added).

So Jesus' blood also is our authority in evangelism praying while we strive to rescue those Satan still has captive in his kingdom all over the world. *No wonder he's terrified of the blood of Jesus.*

BIND SATAN

Mark 3:27 gives us some solid advice for our battle for souls with Satan. If we are to rescue captives from Satan's kingdom, we must first learn to use the *authority of the name and blood of Jesus and bind him.*

But no one can enter the strong man's house and plunder his property unless he first binds the strong man, and then he will plunder his house.

THE VICTORY IS OURS

I frequently picture Jesus' blood flowing against Satan through a person, a room, or a building—dislodging him as it flows, unstoppable. Satan cannot stand against that power.

Sometimes, feeling Satan is smugly ignoring me, I sharply say, "Satan, are you listening? I'm claiming the blood and name of *Jesus!*"

Satan and his hierarchy's absolute ineffectiveness against us is powerfully declared in Romans 8:35-39.

> Who shall separate us from the love of Christ? Shall tribulation, or distress, or persecution, or famine, or nakedness, or peril, or sword? . . . But in all these things we overwhelmingly conquer through Him who loved us. For I am convinced that neither death, nor life, nor angels, nor principalities, nor things present, nor things to come, nor powers, nor height, nor depth, nor any other created thing shall be able to separate us from the love of God, which is in Christ Jesus our Lord.

OUR POSITION

When Paul wrote the Book of Ephesians, before he taught us about our spiritual battle and God's armor in chapter 6, he made sure we unequivocally understood our position as believers in Jesus first. Here are some of the statements about our position in Jesus from Ephesians:

> Blessed be the God and Father of our Lord Jesus Christ, who had blessed us with every spiritual blessing in *the heavenly places in Christ* (Ephesians 1:3, italics added).

> But God . . . made us alive together with Christ . . . and raised us up with Him, and *seated us with Him in the heavenly places, in Christ Jesus* (Ephesians 2:4-6, italics added).

The "heavenly places" is the place of our current battle with Satan and his demons. But, praise God, we are in that realm *in Christ Jesus* being blessed with every spiritual blessing *in Christ!*

Also our citizenship has been transferred (Colossians 1:13), and now is "in heaven." (See Philippians 3:20-21.) And we are fellow citizens with the "saints" (Ephesians 2:19).

Of course, the most important of all is that Jesus is living *in* us (Colossians 1:27). Don't ever waver. Know your position in Jesus—and know that Satan knows 1 John 4:4 better than you do: "Greater is He [Jesus] that is in you, than he [Satan] that is in the world."

Just after leaving the pastorate with my husband almost twenty years ago, I wrote these words:

> I am now living in that exhilaration of being indwelt (1 John 4:4) by the One who is greater than that one who is in the world, Satan. My experience as a pastor's wife has grown from ignorance and fear to the exhilarating position of being part of the body of the resurrected Victor—feeling not fear but joy, not ignorance but experientially knowing the thrill of victory. Not intimidated by the enemy, Satan, but literally feeling the tingle of possessing Christ's resurrected power over him.
>
> I too, with Christ, find no joy in the battle with the enemy, but (unlike Christ who could look into the future and know there was joy set before Him), I can look back historically to that victory—thus knowing that I too have victory. And joy does come in the morning! I have tasted with Christ the exhilarating joy He must have felt when He, in His resurrected body, stepped forth victorious over Satan—from that battle which forever sealed the doom of Satan and his fallen angels!

Power and authority is ours in the battle of rescuing captives from Satan's kingdom—in the precious, victorious name and blood of Jesus.

THIRTEEN
MOBILIZE FOR ACTION
Matthew 24:14

When will this battling the Prince of Darkness come to an end? Will the whole world forever and ever lie in the power of the wicked one, Satan, as is true now? (1 John 5:19) Is there no hope of getting out of this escalating evil?

Yes, there definitely is hope. But the final and complete end to all of Satan's power on planet Earth cannot come until Jesus comes back to rule with righteousness.

Sometimes I think I can't stand all the violence, terror, and sin around us any more. I was horrified at the look in a surgeon's eyes as he reported on the TV evening news how he had tried to sew up a little four-year-old local girl who had been brutally raped with a stick and left for dead behind a dumpster. I woke in the middle of that night, my pillow soaked with tears, crying out, "Oh, Jesus come quickly! Get us out of all this horrible sin and violence."

The conclusion of the earthly human drama, drenched in evil, is vividly spelled out for us in the Bible. *Jesus is coming back!*

This Jesus who has been taken up from you into heaven, will come in just the same way as you have watched Him go into heaven (Acts 1:11).

Yes, the time for Satan's evil reign will run out. And Jesus will rule with righteousness. Second Peter 3:13 says, "But according to His promise we are looking for new heavens and a new earth, in which righteousness dwells."

And those purchased with Jesus' blood will reign on earth with Him.

Worthy art Thou to take the book, and to break its seals; for Thou wast slain, and didst purchase for God with Thy blood men from every tribe and tongue and people and nation. And Thou hast made them to be a kingdom and priests to our God; *and they will reign upon the earth* (Revelation 5:9-10, italics added).

WHAT IS JESUS WAITING FOR?

Those ruling with Him will include people from every tribe, tongue, people, and nation—so Jesus is waiting for them all to hear about Himself. He is waiting until they hear the good news that He delivers from the kingdom of darkness—into His glorious kingdom. It was Jesus Himself who said, *"And this gospel of the kingdom shall be preached in the whole world for a witness to all the nations, and then the end shall come"* (Matthew 24:14, italics added).

This is not every person, but people. A people group is defined by Dr. Ralph Winter in the "Mission Frontiers" Magazine (August, 1989) as "The largest group within which the Gospel can flow along natural lines without encountering barriers of understanding or acceptance due to culture, language, geography, etc." And Jesus won't come back until they each have heard of Him.

One of the final victory scenes of the drama of planet Earth is vividly described in Revelation 7:9-10. It clearly states there will be people from *every* nation, tribe, people, and tongue on earth there:

After these things I looked, and behold, a great multitude, which no one could count, from *every nation and all tribes and peoples and tongues,* standing before the throne and before the Lamb, clothed in white robes, and palm branches were in their hands; and they cry out with a loud voice, saying, "Salvation to our God who sits on the throne, and to the Lamb."

DON'T BLAME GOD IF JESUS DOESN'T COME

People have been blaming God and laughing at Jesus' *not* coming back since the A.D. 1. Second Peter 3:4 tells us that in the last days mockers will come saying, "Where is the promise of His coming? Ever since the fathers fell asleep, all continues just as it was from the beginning of creation."

God obviously is waiting but for what? Peter explained in verse 9 *why* God is waiting to send Jesus back: "The Lord is not slow about His promise, as some count slowness, but is patient toward you, *not wishing for any to perish* but for all to come to repentance" (2 Peter 3:9, italics added).

So God too wants everybody to have a chance to hear of Jesus before He comes back—and as many as possible to be rescued out of Satan's evil kingdom. God loves them so much that He doesn't want any of them to perish. And He knows all will perish who don't believe on Jesus. (See Revelation 20:15.)

SO WHOSE RESPONSIBILITY IS IT?

If it's not Jesus' or God's, whose responsibility is it? *Ours! Jesus clearly told us who is causing the delay. WE ARE!*

We hold the key to planet Earth's ultimate war. This battle between good and evil, Jesus and Satan, will end only when we have told every people group about Jesus. Matthew 24:14 tells us clearly that then the end of this evil world order will come. Until we Christians have brought the redeeming news of Jesus to Satan's captives in every nation of the world, Jesus won't come back to reign.

In His Great Commission recorded in Matthew and Mark, Jesus emphatically told us to "Go therefore and make disciples of *all* the nations" (Matthew 28:19), and "Go into *all* the world and preach the Gospel to *all* creation" (Mark 16:15, italics added).

Jesus didn't pick out a few affluent nations or ones with a certain color skin. He said *all*.

Jesus won't come back until we have obeyed His last instructions to His followers—and each of us—before He left planet Earth. He explicitly said in Acts 1:8 that we should be witnesses unto Him "even to the *remotest part of the earth*" (italics added).

So What Is Our Part?

Jesus did His part. He alone was worthy to "open the book" because He had purchased for God with His blood the people from every spot on planet earth (Revelation 5:9).

Yes, He did His part on the cross. Jesus did pay the price, not only for our sins, but for the sins of the whole world.

> And He Himself is the propitiation for our sins; and not for ours only, but also for those of the whole world (1 John 2:2).

However, He left our part to us—the applying of His victory on the cross to people. Jesus left to us the task of reaching the citizens of Satan's kingdom with His gift of salvation. *Jesus did not, could not, do that on the cross.*

Forgiveness and justification must come individually as each person hears about and accepts Jesus. Nobody is automatically transferred out of Satan's kingdom into Jesus' kingdom just because Jesus died for all.

Jesus did His part, and He expects us to do ours. And He will come back when we have done our part and told them.

Have Told Them What?

About Jesus! "The Gospel of the kingdom."

Today there is much spreading of the *pagan* "gospels," vying for converts to their brand of religion. But Jesus was talking about *the* true Gospel. Jesus gave us the task of giving people from all nations a chance to get out of the *false religions of the kingdom of the Prince of Darkness* and into His kingdom of light.

There is also the popular "gospel" that a new political system, a new constitution, or a new social order will bring peace to a country. Not so. It is only as people are changed *from within* by new life in Jesus that there will be any *real* peace—from the Prince of Peace. Only as people personally and individually are transferred out of Satan's kingdom will they have the *desire* and *power* to live just and holy lives—which is the *only* thing that can bring real peace.

In 1989 in El Salvador I was speaking to the students at the University of San Salvador while the rebels were exploding bombs in parked cars on the street leading up to that University. With all the electricity in the capital city knocked out by the rebels and the armored tanks poised in the streets, tension was running high. So I reported to those students what I had told the South African students at Wits University the year before—just days before their South African white elections. "It won't do any good ultimately," I told them, "to vote into power a new political regime or draft a new constitution. Your only hope for *real* peace is Jesus!

Then, in that auditorium of that leading university of San Salvador—with the social studies students taking notes for written reports for credit—I asked them a question. "Are you interested in finding that peace and power and new life in Jesus? If so, pray this prayer." As I led them in repenting and accepting Jesus, students all over the room just exploded in prayer accepting Jesus—their only hope!

MOBILIZE FOR ACTION
How can we ever begin to reach the world for Jesus? What are the steps we must take to tell all the people groups, so the evil on planet earth can be solved by Jesus' return?

Here are several definite steps we must take.
● **Be willing to feel God's burden.** Before we can mobilize for action, we must first feel God's burden.

Today it is considered "normal" to be looking out for ourselves rather than for others. So it seems "natural," even "right," that Christians are completely absorbed in making money, finding their own security, keeping their bodies physically fit, and pursuing whatever makes them feel good. Somehow the list of imperatives for our lives doesn't seem to include being burdened for those dying in Satan's kingdom without Jesus.

But Jesus' Great Commission didn't include any of these lifestyle musts. Today the lifestyle of many Christians seems closer to the description of the last days—lovers of self, lovers of money, etc.—in 2 Timothy 3·1-7. Jesus' burden was that our hearts would be broken for the lost just as His was.

But we have to be willing to *accept* that burden. This starts with being willing to be sensitive to the Lord when He tries to show us the lost. It is much easier to shut our eyes as He uses situations and circumstances to awaken us. It is much more comfortable to ignore the needs He flashes across our minds with current world events and local tragedies.

In prayer, we need to ask God to show us *His* burden and our part in it.

On October 23, 1988 at 4:30 A.M. I was begging God to show me my future and to explain what He wanted me to do. Rather than answering directly, God strongly impressed on my mind to "read." He obviously had the answer for me, as He usually does, in the Bible. So I turned to where I was reading devotionally in Luke 15. An extremely deep burden overcame me as I read in verse 4: *"leave the ninety-nine . . . and go after the one which is lost"* (italics added).

I wept as I prayed, "Oh, Father, I see You have called me to win the lost. To go find the lost. Forgive me for wondering, Father."

Then the next summer while again reading the same portion suddenly there was another call from the Lord. It was very strong and clear. *"It is the unreached people groups, Evelyn,"* He said. *"It is not necessarily the big '99' groups."*

I was broken, crying before the Lord. Then, in complete submission of soul, I cried to Him, "Oh, God, take me where *You* want me!"

This was not my first call to reach the lost for Jesus. As a new convert at age nine, I battled in prayer for my lost friends. By fourteen I was reaching lost children by teaching

Sunday School pre-schoolers and Child Evangelism classes with my mother. In 1969 I couldn't stand teaching just Christians in the church any longer, so I started my first neighborhood evangelism Bible study. My call to winning the lost overseas came in 1980 when God said "the world" as I knelt, waiting, in prayer for His direction for the coming year. And He showed me His "hidden mission field." One by one God has sent me to all but one of the continents since then.

But they all have been burdens *from the Lord*—not something somebody told me I was supposed to do. Persistent, unshakable burdens. Jesus was not talking about church or parachurch projects. He was talking about *being burdened for—and winning—the lost out of Satan's evil kingdom*.

God doesn't expect us all to be Billy Grahams. We have only to open our eyes to those lost ones all around us and all around the world: little and big, young and old, affluent and destitute—lost ones!

Perhaps you are excusing yourself from this task because God did not give you the gift of evangelism. You feel, therefore, you do not have to take the responsibility of sharing Jesus. But Jesus' Great Commission was not cancelled in your life because your main gift is not witnessing. Whatever your calling, profession, or talents, Jesus' command to go to all the world as His witness still is for you and for all of us. He expects us to win those to whom we show our mercy and with whom we share our hospitality, teaching, etc.,

When our church in Rockford was involved in the "What Happens When Women Pray" project, we were in for a surprise. I reported to our denominational headquarters that the women who were praying automatically were evangelizing "We are seeing our total church program becoming increasingly evangelistic, not superimposed by programs—but from within the hearts of the workers."

Before starting to write this chapter, I was fearful of just recording cold facts and statistics. So I asked God to give me the burden *He* wanted me to have as I wrote it. And He did. As I read Scripture after Scripture, my heart broke for the lost ones without Jesus. The first several hours I tried to type, I wept so much I couldn't see my word processor screen. I kept having to stop to wipe the tears running uncontrollably down my face. At times I would just bury my head in my hands and weep for a lost world. "Oh, God," I finally cried, "I can't stand it!"

● **Resurrect the "lost doctrine."** There are good, worthwhile causes to which we give our allegiance and efforts. To a greater or lesser degree we invest our time, affection, and finances in helping people with problems: emotional, mental, or physical problems. We involve ourselves sacrificially in fundraising for needy groups of people—or in providing housing or food for them. We teach dysfunctional people how to cope. We work with those in prison or their families. We spend endless hours volunteering in programs to help those addicted to alcohol, drugs, or a perverted lifestyle. We spend years, or perhaps a whole lifetime, in some good charitable cause or in the propagation of an ideology.

These are good. But non-Christians do the same. However, these hurting people have a need that non-Christians cannot see or help. It is their lostness—their eternal destiny with Satan in hell instead of in heaven with Jesus. But sadly, most Christians never see—or do anything about—that number one need either.

If we let those people we have helped all of our lives go to a Christless eternity, we have missed the most important part of helping them. We need to see that, no matter how glaring their present need may be, their greatest need is spiritual.

How much do we *really* care about that person we so lovingly are helping if we *deliberately*, or at least *by default*, send them to a Christless eternity?

Christians all need to resurrect God's lost doctrine—that all those they are helping already are condemned by God. Condemned unless we bring, not just our human resources, but our Jesus to them.

● **Be willing to pay the price.** But we also must be willing to "put down our toys and pick up our swords."

In the spiritual battle with the Prince of Darkness for

souls, Satan doesn't give up his captives easily. We must be willing to do battle for those God lays on our hearts even if it takes more courage than we think we can muster. Even if it means being embarrassed or misunderstood by other Christians. Even if it means going to unlovely places, or unsafe areas or countries. It is being willing to give an invitation to accept Jesus, not because it's "getting back to the good old days" when that was in vogue, but because our hearts are breaking for those in our audiences who are struggling to survive in this evil world and literally going to hell forever.

We have to be willing to put feet to our burdens from the Lord. We must be willing to go—if He sends.

Someone said India is where unfriendly parasites have a field day in the sterile digestive systems of visitors. I remember well not only my own attacks, but also how my husband suffered there and had to return to America leaving me to go alone to the interior to conduct the National Prayer Congress. But I left a piece of my heart there and still long to return. As I struggled with my present invitation to India, I questioned my motives for wanting to go back.

In prayer I said, "Lord, just bulldoze it all clear around me. Let me stand with *no* possible wrong motives between You and me." Waiting until He removed all reasons cluttering my response, I then prayed, "Now Lord, bring to my mind my number one reason for wanting to go to India." Immediately I started to weep as my heart broke over the swarming *lost* multitudes there. My real motive!

● **Weep for the lost.** Until we get to the place that we weep over lost souls, the price to reach them for Jesus will seem too high.

Jesus wept over Jerusalem. When Jesus was warned not to go to Jerusalem because Herod wanted to kill Him, He said He must journey on to that city to be killed. Then He cried, "Oh, Jerusalem, Jerusalem, the city that kills the prophets and stones those sent to her! How often I wanted to gather your children together, just as a hen gathers her brood under her wings, and you would not have it!" (Luke 13:34)

And as Jesus descended the Mount of Olives in His trium

phal entry into Jerusalem, "He saw the city and *wept* over it" (Luke 19:41, italics added). Why? Because they would not believe on Him and be rescued from Satan's kingdom.

Jesus wept because He knew the consequences of their not believing on Him. He knew they would be cast into the lake of fire (Revelation 20:15). And He said those lost ones *themselves would weep eternally* in that place.

> Therefore just as the tares are gathered up and burned with fire, so shall it be at the end of the age. The Son of Man will send forth His angels, and they will gather out of His kingdom all stumbling blocks, and those who commit lawlessness, *and will cast them into the furnace of fire; and in that place there shall be* WEEPING *and gnashing of teeth* (Matthew 13:40-42, italics added).

Do we, like Jesus, love people so much that we too are willing to weep over their eternal destiny in hell? Enough to weep over them in prayer? Enough to go?

> He who believes in the Son has eternal life; but he who does not obey the Son *shall not see life,* but the *wrath of God abides on him* (John 3:36, italics added).

It has been said a Christian is recognized as much by the things that make him weep as by the things that make him rejoice. When we get a new grip on *why* Jesus wept, then perhaps we will weep like He did.

We had a city-wide night of prayer for the Chinese during the Tiananmen Square bloodbath. I brought a visiting professor from a college in China to share in my hour of leading it. He broke our hearts as he told how he had been in concentration and labor camps there for twenty-eight years, frequently with nothing to eat except sweet potatoes—even after they had rotted through the winter.

This diet kept his wife from producing milk for their baby, whose starved body he secretly took out to a field in the middle of the night. When he described digging a shallow grave with a rake, we all wept. We also wept for the students as the tanks rolled over them in Beijing—dying not only without freedom, but many without eternal hope. "Oh, God," we wept, "bring Jesus to them!"

TARGET DATE 2,000 A.D.

A joint effort has been launched by hundreds of major denominations and Christian organizations to actually *reach every language group by the year 2,000*. The major international Christian radio broadcasting organizations have divided up the unreached language groups of the world and aim to reach them all by the year 2,000. Churches and organizations, large and small, are banding together, or working separately, with one goal in mind. Reach all the unreached by 2,000!

It was almost 2,000 years ago when Jesus told His followers to get going to all the unreached. "And you shall be My witnesses both in Jerusalem, and in all Judea and Samaria, and even to the remotest part of the earth" (Acts 1:8).

But we still haven't reached the "uttermost parts of the earth." And the world's population is growing faster than we are making converts to Jesus. We are losing ground.

Can we do it by 2,000? It has been estimated there are over 400 local churches in America for *every* unreached people group in the world. We have 80 percent of all Christian wealth in the world. But only one congregation out of 30 sent one of their own to missions last year. We can—*if we will!*

UNKEPT PROMISES

But plans, goals, and promises won't do it. How many of us, in times of deep emotion and burden, have made sincere commitments to the Lord. Promises we really intended to keep. But days, and years, have passed—along with the urgency of the burden and the remembrance of the promise. How quickly we were once again in "life as usual."

We also make corporate promises in large conventions and church meetings. Church history is full of them. I've been in so many of them—with lots of us weeping and vowing *this* time we *will* do it. We *will* keep *this* promise. But then, years later when we look back, we are appalled at how quickly those promises evaporated into thin air.

Phil Bogosian, staff member at U.S. Center for World Missions of Pasadena, California, wrote startling words at the time of the 1989 Lausanne II Convention in Manila. He recalled the solemn covenant with the Lord at Lausanne I in 1979 made by thousands of global church leaders to pray, develop a simple lifestyle, and sacrifice to reach the over two billion people without a witnessing church.

But, in a prophecy from the Lord, God said that "to this day you have not kept this covenant. You have changed your lifestyle. Yes, you have made it more luxurious." Then the Lord added to him that "millions each year among the unreached are dragged to eternal darkness, while My selfish Church listens comfortably to stirring choir anthems in their elegant, new, air-conditioned buildings." The Lord also said to him that there is "blood dripping from your hands. The blood of perishing millions from unreached tribes and peoples, tongues, and nations" (*Mission Frontiers,* U.S. Center for World Missions, Volume 11, August, 1989).

There have been many similar projects before. "Countdown 1900" had the same goals for the last century as we have for A.D. 2000. But they witnessed the rise—and decline—of their hopes.

Will we keep the promises we are making once again about "Target 2,000"?

MOBILIZE FOR ACTION
After sharing God's burden for the lost, setting goals, and making promises to Him—what can we do to make sure we keep those promises?

Get going! Wherever you are, whatever the breadth of your sphere of influence—do something. Now!

Take off your pajamas and put on your armor. Mobilize for action! "Awake, sleeper, and arise from the dead" (Ephesians 5:14).

What ultimate good does it do to teach our Sunday School

or Bible classes if we let our pupils continue on their way to hell? What good does it do to teach marriage enrichment seminars and not give the couple the power to live holy lives—with Jesus in them? Or what good are lifestyle improvement workshops without first getting them transferred out of Satan's evil clutches?

Get going! Plan, pray, and work at getting everybody in your sphere of influence transferred out of Satan's kingdom as quickly as possible. Use every means possible. Expend every bit of energy necessary. But get going!

NO REGRETS

The woman who drove me to the airport after a state-wide denominational convention confided she was devastated by guilt and grief as she realized for the first time that day what she had done to her husband. He had been a non-Christian alcoholic, but she had been a Christian all their married life. She had helped him through many programs and near-death experiences, but she never had shared Jesus with him. She shuddered that her husband now was in a Christless eternity since a recent fatal heart attack. "I promised God today," she said with determination, "that I will *never* miss another opportunity to share Jesus with those I love!"

Earlier that day she, with others, had filled out our little questionnaire which asked:

---

1. Date of last time you were the primary influence in somebody's accepting Jesus as Saviour and Lord.

2. How many have you led to Jesus the last 10 years?

Would you dare fill in that questionnaire?

Then the questionnaire asked if they would promise God, with His help, to do their best to win *one person* to Jesus in the next year. When we asked all those who marked "yes" to come forward to their leadership to pray for them, commissioning them for their new task, we were shocked. Instead of the expected few, every single person in the whole room came forward and promised God to win at least one person to Jesus in the next year.

The session ended in a very moving sight. Instead of the leadership laying hands on a few, we all "commissioned each other" by putting our hands on each other's shoulders and praying for power to witness, as well as for faithfulness to keep our promise.

In India our host was Dr. John Richard, the director of the Evangelical Fellowship of India. With his heart breaking for the lost he stated, accurately, that approximately a third of the world's population has never even *heard* the name of Christ, while another third has never really had a valid opportunity for the Gospel to be clearly explained to them.

Time is running out. At that last great celebration when time *has* run out, how will we feel? Will we be devastated by our neglect—longing to go back for another chance?

When Christ comes back, will we be horrified at a lifestyle that has ignored those near us, and around the world, who needed to be rescued from Satan's kingdom? Will we shrink away from looking into Jesus' eyes?

> And now, little children, abide in Him, so that when He appears, we may have confidence and not shrink away from Him in shame at His coming (1 John 2:28).

Jesus will descend from heaven with a shout, the voice of the archangel, and the trumpet of God, as we are caught up to meet the Lord in the air (1 Thessalonians 4:16-17). But will triumph be dimmed by regrets as we see all those left behind whom we *could* have reached?

GET GOING—BUT NOT WITHOUT POWER

Jesus sent His disciples to the uttermost parts of the world—but not without the Holy Spirit (Acts 1:8). He knew their battles would not be with flesh and blood but supernatural, so they would need the Holy Spirit's power. Jesus' last command recorded by Luke was not "go" but "wait until."

> You are witnesses of these things . . . but you are to stay in the city until you are clothed with power from on high (Luke 24:48-49).

And Jesus' disciples did wait in prayer for ten days. Then, after the Holy Spirit had come, they went—filled with power. And Peter could say that this was what had been spoken of through the Prophet Joel: To God's bondslaves, both men and women, He would pour out His Spirit—and they would prophesy (Acts 2:18). And that very first day 3,000 were transferred out of Satan's kingdom into Jesus' kingdom!

Peter must have been chafing at the bit to tell that he had just seen the risen Lord ascend back to heaven in the clouds. But he did wait. I wonder how many souls would have been saved that first day if Peter had not waited for power.

This is waiting to be filled with the power of the Holy Spirit *before we go*. Why? Because the Gospel does not come "in word only, but also in power and in the Holy Spirit and with full conviction" (1 Thessalonians 1:5). It is not our persuasive words, but the power of God that brings conviction to souls needing to be rescued from Satan's kingdom.

Even Paul said it was His (Christ's) power that was mightily working within him—not his own (Colossians 1:29).

Where is our waiting until we have been clothed with power? When will we learn that our frail human power will not do it against the Prince of Darkness, Satan?

GO THROUGH OUR OPEN DOORS

Through the centuries God has opened up huge doors for the advancement of the Gospel. And, just now, an unbelievable one has swung open in Europe. After sixteen years of trying to keep people isolated from Jesus in Godless communism, the Berlin Wall has opened up.

Communism, as I write, is crumbling before our eyes. There is an open door for the Gospel we haven't seen for over forty years. But as thousands eagerly stream into West

Germany, searching for values to replace their old ones, what are they finding? Jesus? No. Only 1 percent of West Germans go to church. The occult, from Satan, has engulfed most of western Europe.

Millions there are searching for answers as they find themselves in an ideological void. It is like Japan's void after World War II when most realized their emperor could not be God when he had been defeated in war. But today, as then, we are letting the vacuum largely be filled with pagan religions, the New Age, and even Satan worship instead of Christianity.

Eighteen months before the Berlin Wall opened, a German pastor, with tears welling up in his eyes, told me even the Christians in U.S. military bases in his country rarely bother to share Jesus with his fellow citizens.

But Christ is the only real answer to this ideological void. Only He can fill their emptiness with His power, love, and direction for life. Their only hope is to be transferred out of Satan's kingdom into Jesus' kingdom. New freedom, new material possessions, clothes, food, and even new citizenship will never do it. Jesus is the only one who can bring the abundant life for which the world is so frantically searching.

Life also suddenly is changing drastically in South Africa as unprecedented freedoms also are beginning to emerge there.

What are we going to do about it? How long will these exciting doors stay open? Will we get going and go through them with Jesus?

ALL AROUND US
But there also are the *continual* open doors day after day all around us. These are the *lost ones* in our families, neighborhoods, Sunday School classes, places of employment, schools, and leisure activities.

THE ULTIMATE SOLUTION
Satan's kingdom of evil produces people who not only are *born* in a state of sin, but who are *living* in that state of sin until they are transferred into Jesus' kingdom. They are act-

ing out their owner Satan's diabolical plans for an evil society to one extent or the other—some violently and others just quietly filling their sphere of influence with his godlessness.

In our rapidly deteriorating society of drugs, violence, child abuse, pornography, and lack of ethical behavior, the only hope for improvement is Jesus. Jesus is not only the life-after-death solution, but He also makes His converts into new creations. Then they are eligible to get their lifestyle, not from the Prince of Darkness, but from the Prince of Peace—Jesus!

The ultimate, all-encompassing war of planet earth is the battle with the Prince of Darkness for the captives in his kingdom. It is number one in magnitude, scope, and importance both now and eternally.

However, Jesus gave us the ultimate solution to that ultimate war almost 2,000 years ago. Satan looses his captives one by one as we tell them about Jesus and they accept Him as their Saviour and Lord. "How then shall they call upon Him in whom they have not believed? And how shall they believe in Him whom they have not heard? And how shall they hear without a preacher? And how shall they preach unless they are sent?" (Romans 10:14-15)

EACH ONE REACH ONE

A simple solution to the evil exploding in our faces here at home is "Each One Reach One." If each one of us would promise God to reach at least one lost person this year—and keep that promise—our homes, neighborhoods, schools, businesses, and nation soon would be swarming with new creations in Jesus—redeemed by His blood, members of His body, with the authority of Jesus' name, and His blood over the evil around them.

And every people group in the uttermost parts of the earth *can* be reached if we, with our nostrils flared in victory, would invade Satan's territory all around the world. We could pray, send, and go with the planet-changing power of Jesus.

And then Jesus could come back to solve forever all the

evil engulfing planet Earth and us.

Yes, we are fighting the ultimate war against the Prince of Darkness. But do we have to sit helplessly by and let Satan win? Do we have to tolerate the devil producing our Godless society? No! The victory is ours! Jesus said: "And upon this rock I will build my church; *and the gates of hell shall not prevai'*